Penny-Pinching

Main Dishes

ALSO BY JOANNA M. LUND

The Healthy Exchanges Cookbook
HELP: The Healthy Exchanges Lifetime Plan
Cooking Healthy with a Man in Mind
Cooking Healthy with Kids in Mind
The Diabetic's Healthy Exchanges Cookbook
The Strong Bones Healthy Exchanges Cookbook
The Best of Healthy Exchanges Food Newsletter '92 Cookbook
Notes of Encouragement
It's Not a Diet, It's a Way of Life (audiotape)

Penny-Pinching Main Dishes

A HEALTHY EXCHANGES® COOKBOOK

JoAnna M. Lund

HELPing Others HELP Themselves
the **Healthy Exchanges®** Way™

A Perigee Book

This cookbook is dedicated to the buyers at QVC. They know how to make every penny count, so they only offer top-quality merchandise at reasonable prices. I like to think that my recipes are the same . . . good-tasting food that looks like a million bucks, even though it's stirred up on a piggy bank budget!

Contents

Acknowledgments

I'm so thankful to QVC for helping me spread the word to all of you about my "common folk" healthy recipes and commonsense approach to healthy living. But without the complete support of so many, I couldn't do what I do. For doing "whatever needs to be done" and doing it quickly, I want to thank:

John Duff and Barbara O'Shea from Putnam and Paula Piercy and Karen Foner from QVC for asking me to "do it all over again." Being chosen as a Today's Special Value last year is one of the greatest honors my recipes will ever receive. Then, to get to come back this year with another set of books—my feelings go beyond words.

Angela Miller and Coleen O'Shea, for helping me "think my future" and in doing so, helping me carve out the time to do what I love to do . . . create my recipes and write my words.

Shirley Morrow, Laura Powell, and Janelle Davis, for typing, typing, and typing some more. You'd think that by now I'd have learned to spell!

Rita Ahlers, Dee Ewing, and Janis Jackson, for helping me test and retest the recipes. Yes, it's fun, but it's also work, especially when it comes time to do the dishes.

Lori Hansen, for calculating the nutrient values of the recipes. It's a good thing she loves the computer as much as I love creating.

Rose Hoenig, R.D., L.D., for reviewing the recipes and calculating the Diabetic Exchanges. Even though she's busy, she finds the quality time needed to give my recipes the "okay" before I share them with others.

Barbara Alpert, for helping me organize my material so it's easier for everyone not only to use the recipes but also to read the books. I don't think I could find a better writing partner in all of "recipe land."

Cliff Lund, my Truck Drivin' Man and taste tester. He lets me know in no uncertain terms what he likes and what he doesn't like. And he likes these recipes!

Everyone who stopped in at JO's Kitchen Cafe for lunch while we were testing and was asked to sample a new dish. Some remarked that we were giving them the "tips," instead of the other way around.

God, for giving me the talent to create my "common folk" healthy recipes and to write in my "Grandma Moses" style. When I was given a lemon, He showed me how to make lemonade.

Penny-Pinching

Main Dishes

Economy Size May Not Be the Economy Buy!

A re you surprised to read that in a cookbook dedicated to inexpensive dishes? It's advice that may be well worth taking!

If your family consists of one or two people, or if you live in a small apartment with a small refrigerator and an even smaller freezer compartment, why reach for the giant economy size? If you throw away food because your family can't consume it by the expiration date, or because it's covered with freezer burn, what have you saved?

I can think of few worse tasks than finally getting around to cleaning out the refrigerator and throwing away food that can't be identified. You peer into a plastic container and wonder what that dried-up glob could possibly be. It's certainly not appetizing anymore! And it also represents wasted money from your food budget.

One of the best investments you can make if you're committed to cooking on a budget is a roll of masking tape and a permanent black marker. When you put your leftovers away, tear off a piece of tape, stick it firmly down, and write on it the date and what you've placed in the container. Then, instead of throwing out so much food, you'll be able to make the most of whatever you prepare by making sure it's served in a timely fashion.

How can you tell what really saves you money when you're shopping for food? Here's one example. Cheap meat isn't as cheap as it appears. Take hamburger, for instance. It's no secret that a pound of extra-lean (90 to 95 percent lean) ground beef costs at least 75 cents to a dollar more than regular ground beef. But, by the time the lower-priced (and higher-fat) beef is cooked, only a small amount of meat is left floating around in a pan of grease! When extra-lean beef is browned, the shrinkage is almost nil. At most, you might get four real-world servings out of a pound of cheap ground beef, while a pound of extra-lean will serve six or eight. In the final analysis, the cost per serving is cheaper when you purchase the higher-priced meat. (And, it's better for your health, too!) This makes sense, even if math was always your worst subject!

The bottom line when it comes to budgeting is this: economize in ways that make *cents* for you, not for your mother-in-law or your next-door neighbor. If you visit a wholesale shopping club and they're selling cases of chunky tomato sauce, and you *know* that you use chunky tomato sauce at least three times a week, *and* you've got room in your cabinets or closets, then that's an economy purchase that works for you. But what if your local market is having a sale on half gallons of skim milk? You're not a big fan of milk, except for the half cup you pour on your cereal a few mornings a week. You'd rather get your calcium by eating yogurt or making soups with evaporated skim milk. So think clearly for a minute—Can you consume an entire half gallon before it goes bad? I don't think so. If you purchase it, you seem to be saving money, but you're actually wasting it.

My favorite way to economize on groceries is simple: I know the brands I use (see the chapter "A Peek into My Pantry and My Favorite Brands" for more on this) and I keep a little list in my purse of what I usually pay for them. When I'm reading the local paper and I notice that one of "my" brands is on sale, I make a note to pick up more than my usual quantity.

Another method involves the size of the packages I buy. I use loads of Carnation nonfat milk powder, so I buy it in the largest size they sell. But I buy the kind of box that lets you pour it instead of the big box filled with one-quart packages. With all the recipe testing I do, that kind of packaging doesn't work for me, even if it might save me a few cents.

Always remember that different products stay fresh for different lengths of time. I can buy a lot of Keebler piecrusts at once because I'm always testing recipes and I know I'll use them up fast. But if you make one pie a week, then it probably isn't a good idea for you to buy piecrusts by the dozen, even if they're on sale. Most canned goods have a long shelf life, so buy whatever you can comfortably store, but if you find yourself tripping over cartons of canned corn or boxes of Bisquick, you may have tried to over-economize! Don't allow the prospect of saving money crowd you out of your apartment or make it impossible to park your car in your garage. (Don't laugh—I know people who've done this!)

You'll find that most of my recipes were created with the budgets of real people in mind. And of course, if there's a special on your favorite fish or meat, that's a perfect time to try a few new dishes that feature it. But just as I want you to live healthy for the rest of your life, I hope you'll develop food budget wisdom that will work for a lifetime. It's a skill worth learning, I promise you. S-t-r-e-t-c-h-i-n-g your food dollar without sacrificing good health or good taste will convince everyone you know that you're a miracle worker!

Dear Friends,

People often ask me why I include the same general information at the beginning of all my cookbooks. If you've seen any of my other books, you'll know that my "common folk" recipes are just one part of the Healthy Exchanges picture. You know that I firmly believe—and say so whenever and wherever I can—that *Healthy Exchanges is not a diet, it's a way of life!* That's why I include the story of Healthy Exchanges in every book, because I know that the tale of my struggle to lose weight and regain my health is one that speaks to the hearts of many thousands of people. And because Healthy Exchanges is not just a collection of recipes, I always include the wisdom that I've learned from my own experiences and the knowledge of the health and cooking professionals I meet. Whether it's learning about nutrition or making shopping and cooking easier, no Healthy Exchanges book would be complete without features like "A Peek into My Pantry" or "JoAnna's Ten Commandments of Successful Cooking."

Even if you've read my other books you still might want to skim the following chapters—you never know when I'll slip in a new bit of wisdom or suggest a new product that will make your journey to health an easier and tastier one. If you're sharing this book with a friend or family member, you'll want to make sure they read the following pages before they start stirring up the recipes.

If this is the first book of mine that you've read, I want to welcome you with all my heart to the Healthy Exchanges Family. (And, of course, I'd love to hear your comments or questions. See the back of this book for my mailing address . . . or come visit if you happen to find yourself in DeWitt, Iowa—just ask anybody for directions to Healthy Exchanges!)

JoAnna

JoAnna M. Lund

and Healthy

Exchanges

Food is the first invited guest to every special occasion in every family's memory scrapbook. From baptism to graduation, from weddings to wakes, food brings us together.

It wasn't always that way at our house. I used to eat alone, even when my family was there, because while they were dining on real food, I was always nibbling at whatever my newest diet called for. In fact, for twenty-eight years I called myself the diet queen of DeWitt, Iowa.

I tried every diet I ever heard of, every one I could afford, and every one that found its way to my small town in eastern Iowa. I was willing to try anything that promised to "melt off the pounds," determined to deprive my body in every possible way in order to become thin at last.

I sent away for expensive "miracle" diet pills. I starved myself on the Cambridge Diet and the Bahama Diet. I gobbled Ayds diet candies, took thyroid pills, fiber pills, prescription and over-the-counter diet pills. I went to endless weight-loss support group meetings—but I somehow managed to turn healthy programs such as Overeaters Anonymous, Weight Watchers, and TOPS into unhealthy diets . . . diets I could never follow for more than a few months.

I was determined to discover something that worked long-term, but each new failure increased my desperation that I'd never find it.

I ate strange concoctions and rubbed on even stranger potions. I tried liquid diets like Slimfast and Metrecal. I agreed to be hypnotized. I tried reflexology and even had an acupuncture device stuck in my ear!

Does my story sound a lot like yours? I'm not surprised. No wonder the weight-loss business is a billion-dollar industry!

Every new thing I tried seemed to work—at least at first. And losing that first five or ten pounds would get me so excited, I'd believe that this new miracle diet would, finally, get my weight off for keeps.

Inevitably, though, the initial excitement wore off. The diet's routine and boredom set in, and I quit. I shoved the pills to the back of the medicine chest; pushed the cans of powdered shake mix to the rear of the kitchen cabinets; slid all the program materials out of sight under my bed; and once more I felt like a failure.

Like most dieters, I quickly gained back the weight I'd lost each time, along with a few extra "souvenir" pounds that seemed always to settle around my hips. I'd done the diet-lose-weight-gain-it-all-back "yo-yo" on the average of once a year. It's no exaggeration to say that over the years I've lost 1,000 pounds—and gained back 1,150 pounds.

Finally, at the age of 46 I weighed more than I'd ever imagined possible. I'd stopped believing that any diet could work for me. I drowned my sorrows in sacks of cake donuts and wondered if I'd live long enough to watch my grandchildren grow up.

Something had to change.

I had to change.

Finally, I did.

I'm just over 50 now—and I'm 130 pounds less than my all-time high of close to 300 pounds. I've kept the weight off for more than six years. I'd like to lose another ten pounds, but I'm not obsessed about it. If it takes me two or three years to accomplish it, that's okay.

What I *do* care about is never saying hello again to any of those unwanted pounds I said good-bye to!

How did I jump off the roller coaster I was on? For one thing, I finally stopped looking to food to solve my emotional problems. But what really shook me up—and got me started on the path that changed my life—was Operation Desert Storm in early 1991. I sent three children off to the Persian Gulf War—my son-in-law, Matt, a medic in Special Forces; my daughter, Becky, a full-time college student and member of a medical unit in the Army Reserve; and my son, James, a member of the Inactive Army Reserve reactivated as a chemicals expert.

Somehow, knowing that my children were putting their lives on the line got me thinking about my own mortality—and I knew in my heart the last thing they needed while they were overseas was to get a letter from home saying that their mother was ill because of a food-related problem.

The day I drove the third child to the airport to leave for Saudi Arabia, something happened to me that would change my life for the better—and forever. I stopped praying my constant prayer as a professional dieter, which was simply "Please, God, let me lose ten pounds by Friday." Instead, I began praying, "God, please help me not to be a burden to my kids and my family." I quit praying for what I wanted and started praying for what I needed—and in the process my prayers were answered. I couldn't keep the kids safe—that was out of my hands—but I could try to get healthier to better handle the stress of it. It was the least I could do on the home front.

That quiet prayer was the beginning of the new JoAnna Lund. My initial goal was not to lose weight or create healthy recipes. I only wanted to become healthier for my kids, my husband, and myself.

Each of my children returned safely from the Persian Gulf War. But something didn't come back—the 130 extra pounds I'd been lugging around for far too long. I'd finally accepted the truth after all those agonizing years of suffering through on-again, off-again dieting.

There are no "magic" cures in life.

No "magic" potion, pill, or diet will make unwanted pounds disappear.

I found something better than magic, if you can believe it. When I turned my weight and health dilemma over to God for guidance, a new JoAnna Lund and Healthy Exchanges were born.

I discovered a new way to live my life—and uncovered an unexpected talent for creating easy "common folk" healthy recipes, and sharing my commonsense approach to healthy living. I learned that I could motivate others to change their lives and adopt a positive outlook. I began publishing cookbooks and a monthly food newsletter, and speaking to groups all over the country.

I like to say, "When life handed me a lemon, not only did I make healthy, tasty lemonade, I wrote the recipe down!"

What I finally found was not a quick fix or a short-term diet, but a great way to live well for a lifetime.

I want to share it with you.

Healthy Exchanges®

Weight Loss

Choices™/Exchanges

If you've ever been on one of the national weight-loss programs like Weight Watchers or Diet Center, you've already been introduced to the concept of measured portions of different food groups that make up your daily food plan. If you are not familiar with such a system of weight-loss choices or exchanges, here's a brief explanation. (If you want or need more detailed information, you can write to the American Dietetic Association or the American Diabetes Association for comprehensive explanations.)

The idea of food exchanges is to divide foods into basic food groups. The foods in each group are measured in servings that have comparable values. These groups include Proteins/Meats, Breads/Starches, Vegetables, Fats, Fruits, Skim Milk, Free Foods, and Optional Calories.

Each choice or exchange included in a particular group has about the same number of calories and a similar carbohydrate, protein, and fat content as the other foods in that group. Because any food on a particular list can be "exchanged" for any other food in that group, it makes sense to call the food groups *exchanges* or *choices*.

I like to think we are also "exchanging" bad habits and food choices for good ones!

By using Weight Loss Choices™ or exchanges you can choose from a variety of foods without having to calculate the nutrient value of each one. This makes it easier to include a wide variety of foods in your daily menus and gives you the opportunity to tailor your choices to your unique appetite.

If you want to lose weight, you should consult your physician or other weight-control expert regarding the number of servings that would be best for you from each food group. Since men generally require more calories than women, and since the requirements for growing children and teenagers differ from those for adults, the right number of exchanges for any one person is a personal decision.

I have included a suggested plan of weight-loss choices in the pages following the exchange lists. It's a program I used to lose 130 pounds, and it's the one I still follow today.

(If you are a diabetic or have been diagnosed with heart problems, it is best to meet with your physician before using this or any other food program or recipe collection.)

Food Group Weight Loss Choices™/Exchanges

Not all food group exchanges are alike. The ones that follow are for anyone who's interested in weight loss or maintenance. Diabetic exchanges are calculated by the American Diabetic Association, and information about them is provided in *The Diabetic's Healthy Exchanges Cookbook* (Perigee Books).

Every Healthy Exchanges recipe provides calculations in three ways:

- Weight Loss Choices/Exchanges

- Calories, Fat, Protein, Carbohydrates, and Fiber Grams, and Sodium in milligrams

- Diabetic Exchanges calculated for me by a Registered Dietitian

Healthy Exchanges recipes can help you eat well and recover your health, whatever your health concerns may be. Please take a few minutes to review the exchange lists and the suggestions that follow on how to count them. You have lots of great eating in store for you!

Proteins
Meat, poultry, seafood, eggs, cheese, and legumes. One exchange of

Protein is approximately 60 calories. Examples of one Protein choice or exchange:

> 1 ounce cooked weight of lean meat, poultry, or seafood
> 2 ounces white fish
> 1½ ounces 97% fat-free ham
> 1 egg (limit to no more than 4 per week)
> ¼ cup egg substitute
> 3 egg whites
> ¾ ounce reduced-fat cheese
> ½ cup fat-free cottage cheese
> 2 ounces cooked or ¾ ounce uncooked dry beans
> 1 tablespoon peanut butter (also count 1 fat exchange)

Breads

Breads, crackers, cereals, grains, and starchy vegetables. One exchange of Bread is approximately 80 calories. Examples of 1 Bread choice or exchange:

> 1 slice bread or 2 slices reduced-calorie bread (40 calories or less)
> 1 roll, any type (1 ounce)
> ½ cup cooked pasta or ¾ ounce uncooked (scant ½ cup)
> ½ cup cooked rice or 1 ounce uncooked (⅓ cup)
> 3 tablespoons flour
> ¾ ounce cold cereal
> ½ cup cooked hot cereal or ¾ ounce uncooked (2 tablespoons)
> ½ cup corn (kernels or cream-style) or peas
> 4 ounces white potato, cooked, or 5 ounces uncooked
> 3 ounces sweet potato, cooked, or 4 ounces uncooked
> 3 cups air-popped popcorn
> 7 fat-free crackers (¾ ounce)
> 3 (2½-inch squares) graham crackers
> 2 (¾-ounce) rice cakes or 6 mini
> 1 tortilla, any type (6-inch diameter)

Fruits

All fruits and fruit juices. One exchange of Fruit is approximately 60 calories. Examples of one Fruit choice or exchange:

> 1 small apple or ½ cup slices
> 1 small orange
> ½ medium banana

¾ cup berries (except strawberries and cranberries)
1 cup strawberries or cranberries
½ cup canned fruit, packed in fruit juice or rinsed well
2 tablespoons raisins
1 tablespoon spreadable fruit spread
½ cup apple juice (4 fluid ounces)
½ cup orange juice (4 fluid ounces)
½ cup applesauce

Skim Milk

Milk, buttermilk, and yogurt. One exchange of Skim Milk is approximately 90 calories. Examples of one Skim Milk choice or exchange:

1 cup skim milk
½ cup evaporated skim milk
1 cup low-fat buttermilk
¾ cup plain fat-free yogurt
⅓ cup nonfat dry milk powder

Vegetables

All fresh, canned, or frozen vegetables other than the starchy vegetables. One exchange of Vegetable is approximately 30 calories. Examples of one Vegetable choice or exchange:

½ cup vegetable
¼ cup tomato sauce
1 medium fresh tomato
½ cup vegetable juice

Fats

Margarine, mayonnaise, vegetable oils, salad dressings, olives, and nuts. One exchange of fat is approximately 40 calories. Examples of one Fat choice or exchange:

1 teaspoon margarine or 2 teaspoons reduced-calorie margarine
1 teaspoon butter
1 teaspoon vegetable oil
1 teaspoon mayonnaise or 2 teaspoons reduced-calorie mayonnaise
1 teaspoon peanut butter
1 ounce olives
¼ ounce pecans or walnuts

Free Foods

Foods that do not provide nutritional value but are used to enhance the taste of foods are included in the Free Foods group. Examples of these are spices, herbs, extracts, vinegar, lemon juice, mustard, Worcestershire sauce, and soy sauce. Cooking sprays and artificial sweeteners used in moderation are also included in this group. However, you'll see that I include the caloric value of artificial sweeteners in the Optional Calories of the recipes.

You may occasionally see a recipe that lists "free food" as part of the portion. According to the published exchange lists, a free food contains fewer than 20 calories per serving. Two or three servings per day of free foods/drinks are usually allowed in a meal plan.

Optional Calories

Foods that do not fit into any other group but are used in moderation in recipes are included in Optional Calories. Foods that are counted in this way include sugar-free gelatin and puddings, fat-free mayonnaise and dressings, reduced-calorie whipped toppings, reduced-calorie syrups and jams, chocolate chips, coconut, and canned broth.

Sliders™

These are 80 Optional Calorie increments that do not fit into any particular category. You can choose which food group to *slide* these into. It is wise to limit this selection to approximately three to four per day to ensure the best possible nutrition for your body while still enjoying an occasional treat.

Sliders™ may be used in either of the following ways:

1. If you have consumed all your Protein, Bread, Fruit, or Skim Milk Weight Loss Choices for the day, and you want to eat additional foods from those food groups, you simply use a Slider. It's what I call "healthy horse trading." Remember that Sliders may not be traded for choices in the Vegetables or Fats food groups.

2. Sliders may also be deducted from your Optional Calories for the day or week. ¼ Slider equals 20 Optional Calories; ½ Slider equals 40 Optional Calories; ¾ Slider equals 60 Optional Calories; and 1 Slider equals 80 Optional Calories.

Healthy Exchanges® Weight Loss Choices™

My original Healthy Exchanges program of Weight Loss Choices™ was based on an average daily total of 1,400 to 1,600 calories per day. That was what I determined was right for my needs, and for those of most women. Because men require additional calories (about 1,600 to 1,900), here are my suggested plans for women and men. *(If you require more or fewer calories, please revise this plan to meet your individual needs.)*

Each day, women should plan to eat:

2 Skim Milk servings, 90 calories each
2 Fat servings, 40 calories each
3 Fruit servings, 60 calories each
4 Vegetable servings or more, 30 calories each
5 Protein servings, 60 calories each
5 Bread servings, 80 calories each

Each day, men should plan to eat:

2 Skim Milk servings, 90 calories each
4 Fat servings, 40 calories each
3 Fruit servings, 60 calories each
4 Vegetable servings or more, 30 calories each
6 Protein servings, 60 calories each
7 Bread servings, 80 calories each

Young people should follow the program for men but add 1 Skim Milk serving for a total of 3 servings.

You may also choose to add up to 100 Optional Calories per day, and up to 21 to 28 Sliders per week at 80 calories each. If you choose to include more Sliders in your daily or weekly totals, deduct those 80 calories from your Optional Calorie "bank."

A word about **Sliders™:** These are to be counted toward your totals after you have used your allotment of choices of Skim Milk, Protein, Bread, and Fruit for the day. By "sliding" an additional choice into one of these groups, you can meet your individual needs for that day. Sliders are especially helpful when traveling, stressed-out, eating out, or for special events. I often use mine so I can enjoy my favorite Healthy Exchanges desserts. Vegetables are not to be counted as Sliders. Enjoy as many Vegetable choices as you need to feel satisfied. Because we want to limit our fat intake to moderate amounts, additional Fat choices should not be counted as Sliders. If you choose to include more fat on an *occasional* basis, count the extra choices as Optional Calories.

Keep a daily food diary of your Weight Loss Choices, checking off what you eat as you go. If, at the end of the day, your required selections are not 100 percent accounted for, but you have done the best you can, go to bed with a clear conscience. There will be days when you have ¼ Fruit or ½ Bread left over. What are you going to do—eat two slices of an orange or half a slice of bread and throw the rest out? I always say that "nothing in life comes out exact." Just do the best you can . . . *the best you can.*

Try to drink at least eight 8-ounce glasses of water a day. Water truly is the "nectar" of good health.

As a little added insurance, I take a multivitamin each day. It's not essential, but if my day's worth of well-planned meals "bites the dust" when unexpected events intrude on my regular routine, my body still gets its vital nutrients.

The calories listed in each group of choices are averages. Some choices within each group may be higher or lower, so it's important to select a variety of different foods instead of eating the same three or four all the time.

Use your Optional Calories! They are what I call "life's little extras." They make all the difference in how you enjoy your food and appreciate the variety available to you. Yes, we can get by without them, but do you really want to? Keep in mind that you should be using all your daily Weight Loss Choices first to ensure you are getting the basics of good nutrition. But I guarantee that Optional Calories will keep you from feeling deprived—and help you reach your weight-loss goals.

Sodium, Fat, Cholesterol, and Processed Foods

A re Healthy Exchanges ingredients really healthy? When I first created Healthy Exchanges, many people asked about sodium, about whether it was necessary to calculate the percentage of fat, saturated fat, and cholesterol in a healthy diet, and about my use of processed foods in many recipes. I researched these questions as I was developing my program, so you can feel confident about using the recipes and food plan.

Sodium

Most people consume more sodium than their bodies need. The American Heart Association and the American Diabetes Association recommend limiting daily sodium intake to no more than 3,000 milligrams per day. If your doctor suggests you limit your sodium even more, then *you really must read labels.*

Sodium is an essential nutrient and should not be completely eliminated. It helps to regulate blood volume and is needed for normal daily muscle and nerve functions. Most of us, however, have no trouble getting "all we need" and then some.

As with everything else, moderation is my approach. I rarely ever have salt in my list as an added ingredient. But if you're especially sodium-sensitive, make the right choices for you—and save high-sodium foods such as sauerkraut for an occasional treat.

I use lots of spices to enhance flavors, so you won't notice the absence of salt. In the few cases where it is used, salt is vital for the success of the recipe, so please don't omit it.

When I do use an ingredient high in sodium, I try to compensate by using low-sodium products in the remainder of the recipe. Many fat-free products are a little higher in sodium to make up for any loss of flavor that disappeared along with the fat. But when I take advantage of these fat-free, higher-sodium products, I stretch that ingredient within the recipe, lowering the amount of sodium per serving. A good example is my use of fat-free and reduced-sodium canned soups. While the suggested number of servings per can is 2, I make sure my final creation serves at least 4 and sometimes 6. So the soup's sodium has been "watered down" from one-third to one-half of the original amount.

Even if you don't have to watch your sodium intake for medical reasons, using moderation is another "healthy exchange" to make on your own journey to good health.

Fat Percentages

We've been told that 30 percent is the magic number—that we should limit fat intake to 30 percent or less of our total calories. It's good advice, and I try to have a weekly average of 15 percent to 25 percent myself. I believe any less than 15 percent is really just another restrictive diet that won't last. And more than 25 percent on a regular basis is too much of a good thing.

When I started listing fat grams along with calories in my recipes, I was tempted to include the percentage of calories from fat. After all, in the vast majority of my recipes, that percentage is well below 30 percent This even includes my pie recipes that allow you a realistic serving instead of many "diet" recipes that tell you a serving is one-twelfth of a pie.

Figuring fat grams is easy enough. Each gram of fat equals 9 calories. Multiply fat grams by 9, then divide that number by the total calories to get the percentage of calories from fat.

So why don't I do it? After consulting four registered dietitians for advice, I decided to omit this information. They felt that it's too easy for people to become obsessed by that 30 percent figure, which is after all supposed to be a percentage of total calories over the course of a day or a week. We mustn't feel we can't include a healthy ingredient such as pecans or olives in one recipe just because, on its own, it has more than 30 percent of its calories from fat.

An example of this would be a casserole made with 90 percent lean red meat. Most of us benefit from eating red meat in moderation, as it provides iron and niacin in our diets, and it also makes life more enjoyable for us and those who eat with us. If we *only* look at the percentage of calories from fat in a serving of this one dish, which might be as high as 40 to 45 percent, we might choose not to include this recipe in our weekly food plan.

The dietitians suggested that it's important to consider the total picture when making such decisions. As long as your overall food plan keeps fat calories to 30 percent, it's all right to enjoy an occasional dish that is somewhat higher in fat content. Healthy foods I include in **MODERATION** include 90 percent lean red meat, olives, and nuts. I don't eat these foods every day, and you may not either. But occasionally, in a good recipe, they make all the difference in the world between just getting by (deprivation) and truly enjoying your food.

Remember, the goal is eating in a healthy way so you can enjoy and live well the rest of your life.

Saturated Fats and Cholesterol

You'll see that I don't provide calculations for saturated fats or cholesterol amounts in my recipes. It's for the simple and yet not so simple reason that accurate, up-to-date, brand-specific information can be difficult to obtain from food manufacturers, especially since the way in which they produce food keeps changing rapidly. But once more I've consulted with Registered Dietitians and other professionals and found that, because I use only a few products that are high in saturated fat, and use them in such limited quantities, my recipes are suitable for patients concerned about controlling or lowering cholesterol. You'll also find that whenever I do use one of these ingredients *in moderation*, everything else in the recipe, and in the meals my family and I enjoy, is low in fat.

Processed Foods

Just what *is* processed food, anyway? What do I mean by the term "processed food," and why do I use them when the "purest" recipe developers in Recipe Land consider them "pedestrian" and won't ever use something from a box, container, or can? A letter I received and a passing statement from a stranger made me reflect on what I mean when I refer to processed foods, and helped me reaffirm why I use them in my "common folk" healthy recipes.

If you are like the vast millions who agree with me, then I'm not sharing anything new with you. And if you happen to disagree, that's okay, too. After all, this is America, the Land of the Free. We are blessed to live in a great nation where we can all believe what we want about anything.

A few months go, a woman sent me several articles from various "whole food" publications and wrote that she was wary of processed foods, and wondered why I used them in my recipes. She then scribbled on the bottom of her note, "Just how healthy *is* Healthy Exchanges?" Then, a few weeks later, during a chance visit at a public food event with a very pleasant woman, I was struck by how we all have our own definitions of what processed foods are. She shared with me, in a somewhat self-righteous manner, that she *never* uses processed foods. She only cooked with fresh fruits and vegetables, she told me. Then later she said that she used canned reduced-fat soups all the time! Was her definition different than mine, I wondered? Soup in a can, whether it's reduced in fat or not, still meets my definition of a processed food.

So I got out a copy of my book *HELP: Healthy Exchanges Lifetime Plan*, and reread what I had written back then about processed foods. Nothing in my definition had changed since I wrote that section. I still believe that healthy processed foods, such as canned soups, prepared piecrusts, sugar-free instant puddings, nonfat sour cream, and frozen whipped topping, when used properly, all have a place as ingredients in healthy recipes.

I never use an ingredient that hasn't been approved by either the American Diabetic Association, the American Dietetic Association, or the American Heart Association. Whenever I'm in doubt, I send for their position papers, then ask knowledgeable registered dietitians to explain those papers to me in "street language." I've been assured by all of them that the sugar- and fat-free products I use in my recipes are indeed safe.

If you don't agree, nothing I can say or write will convince you otherwise. But, if you've been using the healthy processed foods and have been concerned about the almost daily hoopla you hear about yet another product that's about the doom of all of us, then just stay with reason. For every product on the grocery shelves, there are those who want you to buy it and there are those who don't, *because they want you to buy their products instead*. So we have to learn to sift the fact from the fiction. Let's take sugar substitutes, for example. In making our own evaluations, we should toss out any information provided by the sugar substitute manufacturers, because they have a vested interest in our buying their products. Likewise, we should toss out any information provided by the sugar industry, because they have a vested interest in our not buying sugar substitutes. Then, if you aren't sure if you can really trust the government or any of its agencies, toss out their data, too. That leaves the three associations I mentioned above. Do you think any of them would say a product is safe if it isn't? Or say a product isn't safe when it is? They have nothing to gain or lose, *other than their integrity*, if they intentionally try to mislead us. That's why I only go to these associations for information concerning healthy processed foods.

I certainly don't recommend that everything we eat comes from a can, box, or jar. I think the best of all possible worlds is to start with the basics: grains such as rice, pasta, or corn. Then, for example, add some raw vegetables and extra-lean meat such as poultry, fish, beef, or pork. Stir in some healthy canned soup or tomato sauce, and you'll end up with something that is not only healthy but tastes so good, everyone from toddlers to great-grandparents will want to eat it!

I've never been in favor of spraying everything we eat with chemicals and I don't believe that all our foods should come out of packages. But I do think we should use the best available healthy processed foods to make cooking easier and food taste better. I take advantage of the good-tasting low-fat and low-sugar products found in any grocery store. My recipes are created for busy people like me, people who want to eat healthily and economically but who still want the food to satisfy their taste buds. I don't expect anyone to visit out-of-the-way health food stores or find the time to cook beans from scratch—*because I don't!* Most of you can't grow fresh food in the backyard and many of you may not have access to farmers' markets or large supermarkets. I want to help you figure out realistic ways to make healthy eating a reality *wherever you live*, or you will not stick to a healthy lifestyle for long.

So if you've been swayed (by individuals or companies with vested interests or hidden agendas) into thinking that all processed foods are bad for you, you may want to reconsider your position. Or if you've been fooling yourself into believing that you *never* use processed foods but regularly reach for that healthy canned soup, stop playing games with yourself—you are using processed foods in a healthy way. And, if you're like me and use healthy processed foods in *moderation*, don't let anyone make you feel ashamed about including these products in your healthy lifestyle. Only *you* can decide what's best for *you* and your family's needs.

Part of living a healthy lifestyle is making those decisions and then getting on with life. Congratulations on choosing to live a healthy lifestyle, and let's celebrate together by sharing a piece of Healthy Exchanges pie that I've garnished with Cool Whip Lite!

JoAnna's Ten Commandments of Successful Cooking

A very important part of any journey is knowing where you are going and the best way to get there. If you plan and prepare before you start to cook, you should reach mealtime with foods to write home about!

1. **Read the entire recipe from start to finish** and be sure you understand the process involved. Check that you have all the equipment you will need *before* you begin.

2. **Check the ingredient list** and be sure you have *everything* and in the amounts required. Keep cooking sprays handy—while they're not listed as ingredients, I use them all the time (just a quick squirt!).

3. **Set out *all*** the ingredients and equipment needed to prepare the recipe on the counter near you *before* you start. Remember that old saying, *A stitch in time saves nine?* It applies in the kitchen, too.

4. **Do as much advance preparation as possible** before actually cooking. Chop, cut, grate, or whatever is needed

to prepare the ingredients and have them ready before you start to mix. Turn the oven on at least ten minutes before putting food in to bake, to allow the oven to preheat to the proper temperature.

5. **Use a kitchen timer** to tell you when the cooking or baking time is up. Because stove temperatures vary slightly by manufacturer, you may want to set your timer for five minutes less than the suggested time just to prevent overcooking. Check the progress of your dish at that time, then decide if you need the additional minutes or not.

6. **Measure carefully.** Use glass measures for liquids and metal or plastic cups for dry ingredients. My recipes are based on standard measurements. Unless I tell you it's a scant or full cup, measure the cup level.

7. **For best results, follow the recipe instructions exactly.** Feel free to substitute ingredients that *don't tamper* with the basic chemistry of the recipe, but be sure to leave key ingredients alone. For example, you could substitute sugar-free instant chocolate pudding for sugar-free butterscotch instant pudding, but if you used a six-serving package when a four-serving package was listed in the ingredients, or you used instant when cook-and-serve is required, you won't get the right result.

8. **Clean up as you go.** It is much easier to wash a few items at a time than to face a whole counter of dirty dishes later. The same is true for spills on the counter or floor.

9. **Be careful about doubling or halving a recipe.** Though many recipes can be altered successfully to serve more or fewer people, *many cannot.* This is especially true when it comes to spices and liquids. If you try to double a recipe that calls for 1 teaspoon pumpkin-pie spice, for example, and you double the spice, you may end up with a too-spicy taste. I usually suggest increasing spices or liquid by 1½ times when doubling a recipe. If it tastes a little bland to you, you can increase the spice to 1¾ times the original amount the next time you prepare the dish. Remember: You can always add more, but you can't take it out after it's stirred in.

The same is true with liquid ingredients. If you wanted to **triple** a recipe like my **Southwestern Meat Loaf** because you were planning to serve a crowd, you might think you should use three times as much of every ingredient. Don't, or you could end up with Southwestern Meat Loaf Soup! The original recipe calls for 1¾ cups of chunky tomato sauce, so I'd suggest using 3½ cups when you **triple** the recipe (or 2¾ cups if you **double** it). You'll still have a good-tasting dish that won't run all over the plate.

10. **Write your reactions next to each recipe once you've served it.** Yes, that's right, I'm giving you permission to write in this book. It's yours, after all. Ask yourself: Did everyone like it? Did you have to add another half teaspoon of chili seasoning to please your family, who like to live on the spicier side of the street? You may even want to rate the recipe on a scale of 1★ to 4★, depending on what you thought of it. (Four stars would be the top rating—and I hope you'll feel that way about many of my recipes.) Jotting down your comments while they are fresh in your mind will help you personalize the recipe to your own taste the next time you prepare it.

My Best Healthy Exchanges Tips and Tidbits

Measurements, General Cooking Tips, and Basic Ingredients

The word *moderation* best describes **my use of fats, sugar substitutes,** and **sodium** in these recipes. Wherever possible, I've used cooking spray for sautéing and for browning meats and vegetables. I also use reduced-calorie margarine and no-fat mayonnaise and salad dressings. Lean ground turkey *or* ground beef can be used in the recipes. Just be sure whatever you choose is at least *90 percent lean*.

I've also included **small amounts of sugar and brown sugar substitutes as the sweetening agent** in many of the recipes. I don't drink a hundred cans of soda a day or eat enough artificially sweetened foods in a 24-hour time period to be troubled by sugar substitutes. But if this is a concern of yours and you *do not* need to watch your sugar intake, you can always replace the sugar substitutes with processed sugar and the sugar-free products with regular ones.

I created my recipes knowing they would also be used by hypoglycemics, diabetics, and those concerned about triglycerides. If you choose to use sugar instead, be sure to count the additional calories.

A word of caution when cooking with **sugar substitutes**: Use saccharin-based sweeteners when **heating or baking**. In recipes that **don't require heat, aspartame** (known as NutraSweet) works well in uncooked dishes but leaves an aftertaste in baked products.

I'm often asked why I use an **8-by-8-inch baking dish** in my recipes. It's for portion control. If the recipe says it serves 4, just cut down the center, turn the dish, and cut again. Like magic, there's your serving. Also, if this is the only recipe you are preparing requiring an oven, the square dish fits into a tabletop toaster oven easily and energy can be conserved.

To make life even easier, **whenever a recipe calls for ounce measurements** (other than raw meats) I've included the closest cup equivalent. I need to use my scale daily when creating recipes, so I've measured for you at the same time.

Most of the recipes are for **4 to 6 servings**. If you don't have that many to feed, do what I do: freeze individual portions. Then all you have to do is choose something from the freezer and take it to work for lunch or have your evening meals prepared in advance for the week. In this way, I always have something on hand that is both good to eat and good for me.

Unless a recipe includes hard-boiled eggs, cream cheese, mayonnaise, or a raw vegetable or fruit, **the leftovers should freeze well**. (I've marked recipes that freeze well with the symbol of a **snowflake✻**.)This includes most of the cream pies. Divide any recipe up into individual servings and freeze for your own "TV" dinners.

Another good idea is **cutting leftover pie into individual pieces and freezing each one separately** in a small Ziploc freezer bag. Then the next time you want to thaw a piece of pie for yourself, you don't have to thaw the whole pie. It's great this way for brown-bag lunches, too. Just pull a piece out of the freezer on your way to work and by lunchtime you will have a wonderful dessert waiting for you.

Unless I specify **"covered" for simmering or baking**, prepare my recipes **uncovered**. Occasionally you will read a recipe that asks you to cover a dish for a time, then to uncover, so read the directions carefully—and to get the best results.

Low-fat cooking spray is another blessing in a Healthy Exchanges kitchen. It's currently available in three flavors . . .

- **OLIVE-OIL FLAVORED** when cooking Mexican, Italian, or Greek dishes

- **BUTTER FLAVORED** when the hint of butter is desired

- **REGULAR** for everything else.

A quick spray of butter flavored makes air-popped popcorn a low-fat taste treat, or try it as a butter substitute on steaming hot corn on the cob. One light spray of the skillet when browning meat will convince you that you're using "old-fashioned fat," and a quick coating of the casserole dish before you add the ingredients will make serving easier and cleanup quicker.

I use reduced-sodium **canned chicken broth** in place of dry bouillon to lower the sodium content. The intended flavor is still present in the prepared dish. As a reduced-sodium beef broth is not currently available (at least not in DeWitt, Iowa), I use the canned regular beef broth. The sodium content is still lower than regular dry bouillon.

Whenever **cooked rice or pasta** is an ingredient, follow the package directions, but eliminate the salt and/or margarine called for. This helps lower the sodium and fat content. It tastes just fine; trust me on this.

Here's another tip: When **cooking rice or noodles**, why not cook extra "for the pot"? After you use what you need, store leftover rice in a covered container (where it will keep for a couple of days). With noodles like spaghetti or macaroni, first rinse and drain as usual, then measure out what you need. Put the leftovers in a bowl covered with water, then store in the refrigerator, covered, until they're needed. Then, measure out what you need, rinse and drain them, and they're ready to go.

Does your **pita bread** often tear before you can make a sandwich? Here's my tip to make them open easily: cut the bread in half, put the halves in the microwave for about 15 seconds, and they will open up by themselves. *Voilà!*

When **chunky salsa** is listed as an ingredient, I leave the degree of "heat" up to your personal taste. In our house, I'm considered a wimp. I go for the "mild" while Cliff prefers "extra-hot." How do we compromise? I prepare the recipe with mild salsa because he can always add a spoonful or two of the hotter version to his serving, but I can't enjoy the dish if it's too spicy for me.

Milk and Yogurt

Take it from me—nonfat dry milk powder is great! I *do not* use it for drinking, but I *do* use it for cooking. Three good reasons why:

(1) It is very **inexpensive**.

(2) It **does not sour** because you use it only as needed. Store the box in your refrigerator or freezer and it will keep almost forever.

(3) You can easily **add extra calcium** to just about any recipe without added liquid. I consider nonfat dry milk powder one of Mother Nature's modern-day miracles of convenience. But do purchase a good national name brand (I like Carnation), and keep it fresh by proper storage.

In many of my pies and puddings, I use nonfat dry milk powder and water instead of skim milk. Usually I call for ⅔ cup nonfat dry milk powder and 1¼ to 1½ cups water or liquid. This way I can get the nutrients of two cups of milk, but much less liquid, and the end result is much creamier. Also, the recipe sets up quicker, usually in 5 minutes or less. So if someone knocks at your door unexpectedly at mealtime, you can quickly throw a pie together and enjoy it minutes later.

You can make your own **"sour cream"** by combining ¾ cup plain fat-free yogurt with ⅓ cup nonfat dry milk powder. What you did by doing this is fourfold: 1) The dry milk stabilizes the yogurt and keeps the whey from separating. 2) The dry milk slightly helps to cut the tartness of the yogurt. 3) It's still virtually fat-free. 4) The calcium has been increased by 100 percent. Isn't it great how we can make that distant relative of sour cream a first kissin' cousin by adding the nonfat dry milk powder? Or, if you place 1 cup of plain fat-free yogurt in a sieve lined with a coffee filter, and place the sieve over a small bowl and refrigerate for about 6 hours, you will end up with a very good alternative for sour cream. To **stabilize yogurt** when cooking or baking with it, just add 1 teaspoon cornstarch to every ¾ cup yogurt.

If a recipe calls for **evaporated skim milk** and you don't have any in the cupboard, make your own. For every ½ cup evaporated skim milk needed, combine ⅓ cup nonfat dry milk powder and ½ cup water. Use as you would evaporated skim milk.

You can also make your own **sugar-free and fat-free sweetened condensed milk** at home. Combine 1⅓ cups nonfat dry milk powder and ½ cup cold water in a 2-cup glass measure. Cover and microwave on HIGH until mixture is hot but *not* boiling. Stir in ½ cup Sprinkle Sweet or Sugar Twin. Cover and refrigerate at least 4 hours. This mixture will keep for up to 2 weeks in the refrigerator. Use in just about any recipe that calls for sweetened condensed milk.

For any recipe that calls for **buttermilk**, you might want to try JO's Buttermilk: Blend one cup of water and ⅔ cup dry milk powder (the nutrients of two cups of skim milk). It'll be thicker than this mixed-up milk usually is, because it's doubled. Add 1 teaspoon white vinegar and stir, then let it sit for at least 10 minutes.

One of my subscribers was looking for a way to further restrict salt intake, and needed a substitute for **cream of mushroom soup**. For many of my recipes, I use Healthy Request Cream of Mushroom Soup, as it is a reduced-sodium product. The label suggests 2 servings per can, but I usually incorporate the soup into a recipe serving at least four. By doing this, I've reduced the sodium in the soup by half again.

But if you must restrict your sodium even more, try making my Healthy Exchanges **Creamy Mushroom Sauce**. Place 1½ cups evaporated skim milk and 3 tablespoons flour in a covered jar. Shake well and pour mixture into a medium saucepan sprayed with butter-flavored cooking spray. Add ½ cup canned sliced mushrooms, rinsed and drained. Cook over medium heat, stirring often, until mixture thickens. Add any seasonings of your choice. You can use this sauce in any recipe that calls for one 10¾-ounce can of cream of mushroom soup.

Why did I choose these proportions and ingredients?

- 1½ cups evaporated skim milk is the amount in one can.

- It's equal to three milk choices or exchanges.

- It's the perfect amount of liquid and flour for a medium cream sauce.

- 3 tablespoons flour is equal to one bread/starch choice or exchange.

- Any leftovers will reheat beautifully with a flour-based sauce, but not with a cornstarch base.

- The mushrooms are one vegetable choice or exchange.

- This sauce is virtually fat-free, sugar-free, and sodium-free.

Proteins

I use eggs in moderation. I enjoy the real thing on an average of three to four times a week. So, my recipes are calculated on using whole eggs. However, if you choose to use egg substitute in place of the egg, the finished product will turn out just fine and the fat grams per serving will be even lower than those listed.

If you like the look, taste, and feel of **hard-boiled eggs** in salads but haven't been using them because of the cholesterol in the yolk, I have a couple of alternatives for you. 1) Pour an 8-ounce carton of egg substitute into a medium skillet sprayed with cooking spray. Cover skillet tightly and cook over low heat until substitute is just set, about 10 minutes. Remove from heat and let set, still covered, for 10 minutes more. Uncover and cool completely. Chop set mixture. This will make about 1 cup of chopped egg. 2) Even easier is to hard-boil "real eggs," toss the yolk away, and chop the white. Either way, you don't deprive yourself of the pleasure of egg in your salad.

In most recipes calling for **egg substitutes**, you can use 2 egg whites in place of the equivalent of 1 egg substitute. Just break the eggs open and toss the yolks away. I can hear some of you already saying, "But that's wasteful!" Well, take a look at the price on the egg substitute package (which usually has the equivalent of 4 eggs in it), then look at the price of a dozen eggs, from which you'd get the equivalent of 6 egg substitutes. Now, what's wasteful about that?

Whenever I include **cooked chicken** in a recipe, I use roasted white meat without skin. Whenever I include **roast beef or pork** in a recipe, I use the loin cuts because they are much leaner. However, most of the time, I do my roasting of all these meats at the local deli. I just ask for a chunk of their lean roasted meat, 6 or 8 ounces, and ask them not to slice it. When I get home, I cube or dice the meat and am ready to use it in my recipe. The reason I do this is threefold: 1) I'm getting just the amount I need without leftovers; 2) I don't have the expense of heating the oven; and 3) I'm not throwing away the bone, gristle, and fat I'd be cutting away from the meat. Overall, it is probably cheaper to "roast" it the way I do.

Did you know that you can make an acceptable meat loaf without using egg for the binding? Just replace every egg with ¼ cup of liquid. You could use beef broth, tomato sauce, even applesauce, to name just a few. For a meat loaf to serve 6, I always use 1 pound of extra-lean ground beef or turkey, 6 tablespoons of dried fine bread crumbs, and ¼ cup of the liquid, plus anything else healthy that strikes my fancy at the time. I mix well and place the mixture in an 8-by-8-inch baking dish or 9-by-5-inch loaf pan sprayed with cooking spray. Bake uncovered at 350 degrees for 35 to 50 minutes (depending on the added ingredients). You will never miss the egg.

Any time you are **browning ground meat** for a casserole and want to get rid of almost all the excess fat, just place the uncooked meat loosely in a plastic colander. Set the colander in a glass pie plate. Place in microwave and cook on HIGH for 3 to 6 minutes (depending on the amount being browned), stirring often. Use as you would for any casserole. You can also chop up onions and brown them with the meat if you want.

Fruits and Vegetables

If you want to enjoy a **"fruit shake"** with some pizzazz, just combine soda water and unsweetened fruit juice in a blender. Add crushed ice. Blend on HIGH until thick. Refreshment without guilt.

You'll see that many recipes use ordinary **canned vegetables**. They're much cheaper than reduced-sodium versions, and once you rinse and drain them, the sodium is reduced anyway. I believe in saving money wherever possible so we can afford the best fat-free and sugar-free products as they come onto the market.

All three kinds of **vegetables—fresh, frozen, and canned—**have their place in a healthy diet. My husband, Cliff, hates the taste of frozen or fresh green beans, thinks the texture is all wrong, so I use canned green beans instead. In this case, canned vegetables have their proper place when I'm feeding my husband. If someone in your family has a similar concern, it's important to respond to it so everyone can be happy and enjoy the meal.

When I use **fruits or vegetables** like apples, cucumbers, and zucchini, I wash them really well and **leave the skin on**. It provides added color, fiber, and attractiveness to any dish. And, because I use processed flour in my cooking, I like to increase the fiber in my diet by eating my fruits and vegetables in their closest-to-natural state.

To help keep **fresh fruits and veggies fresh**, just give them a quick "shower" with lemon juice. The easiest way to do this is to pour purchased lemon juice into a kitchen spray bottle and store in the refrigerator. Then, every time you use fresh fruits or vegetables in a salad or dessert, simply give them a quick spray with your "lemon spritzer." You just might be amazed by how this little trick keeps your produce from turning brown so fast.

The next time you warm canned vegetables such as carrots or green beans, drain and heat the vegetables in ¼ cup beef or chicken broth. It gives a nice variation to an old standby. Here's a simple **white sauce** for vegetables and casseroles without using added fat that can be made by spraying a medium saucepan with butter-flavored cooking spray. Place 1½ cups evaporated skim milk and 3 tablespoons flour in a covered jar. Shake well. Pour into sprayed saucepan and cook over medium heat until thick, stirring constantly. Add salt and pepper to taste. You can also add ½ cup canned drained mushrooms and/or 3 ounces (¾ cup) shredded reduced-fat cheese. Continue cooking until cheese melts.

Zip up canned or frozen green beans with **chunky salsa**: ½ cup to 2 cups beans. Heat thoroughly. Chunky salsa also makes a wonderful dressing on lettuce salads. It only counts as a vegetable, so enjoy.

Another wonderful **South of the Border** dressing can be stirred up by using ½ cup of chunky salsa and ¼ cup fat-free Ranch dressing. Cover and store in your refrigerator. Use as a dressing for salads or as a topping for baked potatoes.

For **gravy** with all the "old time" flavor but without the extra fat, try this almost effortless way to prepare it. (It's almost as easy as opening up a store-bought jar.) Pour the juice off your roasted meat, then set the roast aside to "rest" for about 20 minutes. Place the juice in an uncovered cake pan or other large flat pan (we want the large air surface to speed up the cooling process) and put in the freezer until the fat congeals on top and you can skim it off. Or, if you prefer, use a skimming pitcher purchased at your kitchen gadget store. Either way, measure about 1½ cups skimmed broth and pour into a medium saucepan. Cook over medium heat until heated through, about 5 minutes. In a covered jar, combine ½ cup water or cooled potato broth with 3 tablespoons flour. Shake well. Pour flour mixture into warmed juice. Combine well using a wire whisk. Continue cooking until gravy thickens, about 5 minutes. Season with salt and pepper to taste.

Why did I use flour instead of cornstarch? Because any leftovers will reheat nicely with the flour base and would not with a cornstarch base. Also, 3 tablespoons of flour works out to 1 Bread/Starch exchange. This virtually fat-free gravy makes about 2 cups, so you could spoon about ½ cup gravy on your low-fat mashed potatoes and only have to count your gravy as ¼ Bread/Starch exchange.

Desserts

Thaw **lite whipped topping** in the refrigerator overnight. Never try to force the thawing by stirring or using a microwave to soften. Stirring it will remove the air from the topping that gives it the lightness and texture we want, and there's not enough fat in it to survive being heated.

How can I **frost an entire pie with just ½ cup of whipped topping?** First, don't use an inexpensive brand. I use Cool Whip Lite or La Creme Lite. Make sure the topping is fully thawed. Always spread from the center to the sides using a rubber spatula. This way, ½ cup topping will literally cover an entire pie. Remember, the operative word is *frost*, not pile the entire container on top of the pie!

For a special treat that tastes anything but "diet," try placing **spreadable fruit** in a container and microwave for about 15 seconds. Then pour the melted fruit spread over a serving of nonfat ice cream or frozen yogurt. One tablespoon of spreadable fruit is equal to 1 fruit serving. Some combinations to get you started are apricot over chocolate ice cream, strawberry over strawberry ice cream, or any flavor over vanilla.

Another way I use spreadable fruit is to make a delicious **topping for a cheesecake or angel food cake**. I take ½ cup of fruit and ½ cup Cool Whip Lite and blend the two together with a teaspoon of coconut extract.

Here's a really **good topping** for the fall of the year. Place 1½ cups unsweetened applesauce in a medium saucepan or 4-cup glass measure. Stir in 2 tablespoons raisins, 1 teaspoon apple pie spice, and

2 tablespoons Cary's Sugar Free Maple Syrup. Cook over medium heat on stove or process on HIGH in microwave until warm. Then spoon about ½ cup warm mixture over pancakes, French toast, or fat-free and sugar-free vanilla ice cream. It's as close as you will get to guilt-free apple pie!

A quick yet tasty way to prepare **strawberries for shortcake** is to place about ¾ cup sliced strawberries, 2 tablespoons Diet Mountain Dew, and sugar substitute to equal ¼ cup sugar in a blender container. Process on BLEND until mixture is smooth. Pour mixture into bowl. Add 1¼ cups sliced strawberries and mix well. Cover and refrigerate until ready to serve with shortcake.

The next time you are making treats for the family, try using **unsweetened applesauce** for some or all of the required oil in the recipe. For instance, if the recipe calls for ½ cup cooking oil, use up to the ½ cup in applesauce. It works and most people will not even notice the difference. It's great in purchased cake mixes, but so far I haven't been able to figure out a way to deep-fat fry with it!

Another trick I often use is to include tiny amounts of "real people" food, such as coconut, but extend the flavor by using extracts. Try it—you will be surprised by how little of the real thing you can use and still feel you are not being deprived.

If you are preparing a pie filling that has ample moisture, just line **graham crackers** in the bottom of a 9-by-9-inch cake pan. Pour the filling over the top of the crackers. Cover and refrigerate until the moisture has enough time to soften the crackers. Overnight is best. This eliminates the added **fats and sugars of a piecrust.**

When **stirring fat-free cream cheese to soften it**, use only a sturdy spoon, never an electric mixer. The speed of a mixer can cause the cream cheese to lose its texture and become watery.

Did you know you can make your own **fruit-flavored yogurt**? Mix 1 tablespoon of any flavor of spreadable fruit spread with ¾ cup plain yogurt. It's every bit as tasty and much cheaper. You can also make your own **lemon yogurt** by combining 3 cups plain fat-free yogurt with 1 tub Crystal Light lemonade powder. Mix well, cover, and store in refrigerator. I think you will be pleasantly surprised by the ease, cost, and flavor of this "made from scratch" calcium-rich treat. P.S.: You can make any flavor you like by using any of the Crystal Light mixes—Cranberry? Iced tea? You decide.

Sugar-free puddings and gelatins are important to many of my recipes, but if you prefer to avoid sugar substitutes, you could still prepare the recipes with regular puddings or gelatins. The calories would be higher, but you would still be cooking low-fat.

When a recipe calls for **chopped nuts** (and you only have whole ones), who wants to dirty the food processor just for a couple of tablespoons? You could try to chop them using your cutting board, but be prepared for bits and pieces to fly all over the kitchen. I use "Grandma's food processor." I use the biggest nuts I can find, put them in a small glass bowl, and chop them into chunks just the right size using a metal biscuit cutter.

If you have a **leftover muffin** and are looking for something a little different for breakfast, you can make a "**breakfast sundae**." Crumble the muffin into a cereal bowl. Sprinkle a serving of fresh fruit over it and top with a couple of tablespoons nonfat plain yogurt sweetened with sugar substitute and your choice of extract. The thought of it just might make you jump out of bed with a smile on your face. (Speaking of muffins, did you know that if you fill the unused muffin wells with water when baking muffins, you help ensure more even baking and protect the muffin pan at the same time?) Another muffin hint: Lightly spray the inside of paper baking cups with butter-flavored cooking spray before spooning the muffin batter into them. Then you won't end up with paper clinging to your fresh-baked muffins.

The secret of making **good meringues** without sugar is to use 1 tablespoon of Sprinkle Sweet or Sugar Twin for every egg white, and a small amount of extract. Use ½ to 1 teaspoon for the batch. Almond, vanilla, and coconut are all good choices. Use the same amount of cream of tartar you usually do. Bake the meringue in the same old way. Don't think you can't have meringue pies because you can't eat sugar. You can, if you do it my way. (Remember that egg whites whip up best at room temperature.)

Homemade or Store-Bought?

I've been asked which is better for you: homemade from scratch, or purchased foods. My answer is *both!* They each have a place in a healthy lifestyle, and what that place is has everything to do with you.

Take **piecrusts**, for instance. If you love spending your spare time in the kitchen preparing foods, and you're using low-fat, low-sugar, and reasonably low sodium ingredients, go for it! But if, like so many people, your time is limited and you've learned to read labels, you could be better off using purchased foods.

I know that when I prepare a pie (and I experiment with a couple of pies each week, because this is Cliff's favorite dessert) I use a purchased crust. Why? Mainly because I can't make a good-tasting piecrust that is lower in fat than the brands I use. Also, purchased piecrusts fit my rule of "If it takes longer to fix than to eat, forget it!"

I've checked the nutrient information for the purchased piecrusts against recipes for traditional and "diet" piecrusts, using my computer software program. The purchased crust calculated lower in both fat and calories! I have tried some low-fat and low-sugar recipes, but they just didn't spark my taste buds, or were so complicated you needed an engineering degree just to get the crust in the pie plate.

I'm very happy with the purchased piecrusts in my recipes, because the finished product rarely, if ever, has more than 30 percent of total calories coming from fats. I also believe that we have to prepare foods our families and friends will eat with us on a regular basis and not feel deprived, or we've wasted time, energy, and money.

I could use a purchased "lite" **pie filling**, but instead I make my own. Here I can save both fat and sugar, and still make the filling almost as fast as opening a can. The bottom line: Know what you have to spend when it comes to both time and fat/sugar calories, then make the best decision you can for you and your family. And don't go without an occasional piece of pie because you think it isn't *necessary*. A delicious pie prepared in a healthy way is one of the simple pleasures of life. It's a little thing, but it can make all the difference between just getting by with the bare minimum and living a full and healthy lifestyle.

Many people have experimented with my tip about **substituting applesauce and artificial sweetener for butter and sugar**, but what if you aren't satisfied with the result? One woman wrote to me about a recipe for her grandmother's cookies that called for 1 cup butter and 1½ cups sugar. Well, any recipe that depends on as much butter and sugar as this one does is generally not a good candidate for "healthy exchanges." The original recipe needed a large quantity of fat to produce a crisp cookie just like Grandma made.

Unsweetened applesauce can be used to substitute for vegetable oil with various degrees of success, but not to replace butter, lard, or margarine. If your recipe calls for ½ cup oil or less, and it's a quick bread, muffin, or bar cookie, it should work to replace the oil with applesauce. If the recipe calls for more than ½ cup oil, then experiment with half oil, half applesauce. You've still made the recipe healthier, even if you haven't removed all the oil from it.

Another rule for healthy substitution: Up to ½ cup sugar or less can be replaced by *an artificial sweetener that can withstand the heat of baking*, like Sugar Twin or Sprinkle Sweet. If it requires more than ½ cup sugar, cut the amount needed by 75 percent and use ½ cup sugar substitute and sugar for the rest. Other options: reduce the butter and sugar by 25 percent and see if the finished product still satisfies you in taste and appearance. Or, make the cookies just like Grandma did, realizing they are part of your family's holiday tradition. Enjoy a moderate serving of a couple of cookies once or twice during the season, and just forget about them the rest of the year.

I'm sure you'll add to this list of cooking tips as you begin preparing Healthy Exchanges recipes and discover how easy it can be to adapt your own favorite recipes using these ideas and your own common sense.

A Peek into My Pantry and My Favorite Brands

Everyone asks me what foods I keep on hand and what brands I use. There are lots of good products on the grocery shelves today—many more than we dreamed about even a year or two ago. And I can't wait to see what's out there twelve months from now. The following are my staples and, where appropriate, my favorites *at this time.* I feel these products are healthier, tastier, easy to get—and deliver the most flavor for the least amount of fat, sugar, or calories. If you find others you like as well *or better,* please use them. This is only a guide to make your grocery shopping and cooking easier.

Fat-free plain yogurt (*Yoplait or Dannon*)
Nonfat dry skim milk powder (*Carnation*)
Evaporated skim milk (*Carnation*)
Skim milk
Fat-free cottage cheese
Fat-free cream cheese (*Philadelphia*)
Fat-free mayonnaise (*Kraft*)
Fat-free salad dressings (*Kraft*)
Fat-free sour cream (*Land O Lakes*)
Reduced-calorie margarine (*Weight Watchers, Promise, or Smart Beat*)
Cooking spray:
   Olive-oil flavored and regular (*Pam*)
   Butter flavored for sautéing (*Weight Watchers*)

Butter flavored for spritzing *after* cooking (*I Can't Believe It's Not Butter!*)

Vegetable oil (*Puritan Canola Oil*)

Reduced-calorie whipped topping (*Cool Whip Lite or Cool Whip Free*)

Sugar Substitute
    if no heating is involved (*Equal*)
    if heating is required
        white (*Sugar Twin or Sprinkle Sweet*)
        brown (*Brown Sugar Twin*)

Sugar-free gelatin and pudding mixes (*JELL-O*)

Baking mix (*Bisquick Reduced Fat*)

Pancake mix (*Aunt Jemima Reduced Calorie*)

Reduced-calorie pancake syrup (*Cary's Sugar Free*)

Parmesan cheese (*Kraft fat-free*)

Reduced-fat cheese (*Kraft ⅓ Less Fat*)

Shredded frozen potatoes (*Mr. Dell's*)

Spreadable fruit spread (*Knott's Berry Farm, Smucker's, or Welch's*)

Peanut butter (*Peter Pan reduced-fat, Jif reduced-fat, or Skippy reduced-fat*)

Chicken broth (*Healthy Request*)

Beef broth (*Swanson*)

Tomato sauce (*Hunt's—Chunky and Regular*)

Canned soups (*Healthy Request*)

Tomato juice (*Campbell's Reduced-Sodium*)

Ketchup (*Heinz Light Harvest or Healthy Choice*)

Purchased piecrust
    unbaked (*Pillsbury—from dairy case*)
    graham cracker, butter flavored, or chocolate flavored (*Keebler*)

Crescent rolls (*Pillsbury Reduced Fat*)

Pastrami and corned beef (*Carl Buddig Lean*)

Luncheon meats (*Healthy Choice or Oscar Mayer*)

Ham (*Dubuque 97% fat-free and reduced-sodium or Healthy Choice*)

Frankfurters and Kielbasa sausage (*Healthy Choice*)

Canned white chicken, packed in water (*Swanson*)

Canned tuna, packed in water (*Chicken of the Sea*)

90 to 95 percent lean ground turkey and beef

Soda crackers (*Nabisco Fat-Free*)
Reduced-calorie bread—40 calories per slice or less
Hamburger buns—80 calories each (*Less*)
Rice—instant, regular, brown, and wild
Instant potato flakes (*Betty Crocker Potato Buds*)
Noodles, spaghetti, and macaroni
Salsa (*Chi Chi's Mild Chunky*)
Pickle relish—dill, sweet, and hot dog
Mustard—Dijon, prepared, and spicy
Unsweetened apple juice
Unsweetened applesauce
Fruit—fresh, frozen (no sugar added), or canned in juice
Vegetables—fresh, frozen, or canned
Spices—JO's Spices
Lemon and lime juice (in small plastic fruit-shaped bottles
    found in produce section)
Instant fruit beverage mixes (*Crystal Light*)
Dry dairy beverage mixes (*Nestlé's Quik and Swiss Miss*)
"Ice cream"—*Wells' Blue Bunny sugar- and fat-free*

The items on my shopping list are everyday foods found in just about any grocery store in America. But all are as low in fat, sugar, calories, and sodium as I can find—and that still taste good! I can make any recipe in my cookbooks and newsletters as long as I have my cupboards and refrigerator stocked with these items. Whenever I use the last of any one item, I just make sure I pick up another supply the next time I'm at the store.

If your grocer does not stock these items, why not ask if they can be ordered on a trial basis? If the store agrees to do so, be sure to tell your friends to stop by, so that sales are good enough to warrant restocking the new products. Competition for shelf space is fierce, so only products that sell well stay around.

Shopping The
Healthy
Exchanges Way

Sometimes, as part of a cooking demonstration, I take the group on a field trip to the nearest supermarket. There's no better place to share my discoveries about which healthy products taste best, which are best for you, and which healthy products don't deliver enough taste to include in my recipes.

While I'd certainly enjoy accompanying you to your neighborhood store, we'll have to settle for a field trip *on paper.* I've tasted and tried just about every fat- and sugar-free product on the market, but so many new ones keep coming all the time, you're going to have to learn to play detective on your own. I've turned label reading into an art, but often the label doesn't tell me everything I need to know.

Sometimes you'll find, as I have, that the product with *no* fat doesn't provide the taste satisfaction you require; other times, a no-fat or low-fat product just doesn't cook up the same way as the original product. And some foods, including even the leanest meats, can't eliminate *all* the fat. That's okay, though—a healthy diet should include anywhere from 15 to 25 percent of total calories from fat on any given day.

Take my word for it—your supermarket is filled with lots of delicious foods that can and should be part of your healthy diet for life. Come, join me as we check it out on the way to the checkout!

First stop, the **salad dressing** aisle. Salad dressing is usually a high-fat food, but there are great alternatives available. Let's look first at the regular Ranch dressing—2 tablespoons have 170 calories and

18 grams of fat—and who can eat just 2 tablespoons? Already, that's about half the fat grams most people should consume in a day. Of course, it's the most flavorful too. Now let's look at the low-fat version. Two tablespoons have 110 calories and 11 grams of fat; they took about half of the fat out, but there's still a lot of sugar there. The fat-free version has 50 calories and zero grams of fat, but they also took most of the flavor out. Here's what you do to get it back: add a tablespoon of fat-free mayonnaise, a few more parsley flakes, and about a half teaspoon of sugar substitute to your 2-tablespoon serving. That trick, with the fat-free mayo and sugar substitute, will work with just about any fat-free dressing and give it more of that full-bodied flavor of the high-fat version. Be careful not to add too much sugar substitute—you don't want it to become sickeningly sweet.

I use Kraft fat-free **mayonnaise** at 10 calories per tablespoon to make scalloped potatoes, too. The Smart Beat brand is also a good one.

Before I buy anything at the store, I read the label carefully: the total fat plus the saturated fat; I look to see how many calories are in a realistic serving, and I say to myself, Would I eat that much—or would I eat more? I look at the sodium and I look at the total carbohydrates. I like to check those ingredients because I'm cooking for diabetics and heart patients too. And I check the total calories from fat.

Remember that 1 fat gram equals 9 calories, while 1 protein or 1 carbohydrate gram equals 4 calories.

A wonderful new product is I Can't Believe It's Not Butter! spray, with zero calories and zero grams of fat in four squirts. It's great for your air-popped popcorn. As for **light margarine spread**, beware—most of the fat-free brands don't melt on toast, and they don't taste very good either, so I just leave them on the shelf. For the few times I do use a light margarine I tend to buy Smart Beat Ultra, Promise Ultra, or Weight Watchers Light Ultra. The number-one ingredient in them is water. I occasionally use the light margarine in cooking, but I don't really put margarine on my toast anymore. I use apple butter or make a spread with fat-free cream cheese mixed with a little spreadable fruit instead.

So far, Pillsbury hasn't released a reduced-fat **crescent roll**, so you'll only get one crescent roll per serving from me. I usually make eight of the rolls serve twelve by using them for a crust. The house brands may be lower in fat, but they're usually not as good flavor wise—and don't quite cover the pan when you use them to make a crust. If you're going to use crescent rolls with lots of other stuff on top, then a house brand might be fine.

The Pillsbury French Loaf makes a wonderful **pizza crust** and fills a giant jelly-roll pan. One-fifth of this package "costs" you only 1 gram of fat (and I don't even let you have that much!). Once you use this for your pizza crust, you will never go back to anything else instead. I use it to make calzones too.

I only use Philadelphia fat-free **cream cheese** because it has the best consistency. I've tried other brands, but I wasn't happy with them. Healthy Choice makes lots of great products, but their cream cheese just doesn't work as well with my recipes.

Let's move to the **cheese** aisle. My preferred brand is Kraft ⅓ Less Fat Shredded Cheeses. I will not use the fat-free versions because *they don't melt.* I would gladly give up sugar and fat, but I will not give up flavor. This is a happy compromise. I use the reduced-fat version, I use less, and I use it where your eyes "eat" it, on top of the recipe. So you walk away satisfied and with a finished product that's very low in fat. If you want to make grilled cheese sandwiches for your kids, use the Kraft ⅓ Less Fat cheese slices, and it'll taste exactly like the one they're used to. The fat-free will not.

Some brands have come out with a fat-free **hot dog,** but the ones we've tasted haven't been very good. So far, among the low-fat brands, I think Healthy Choice tastes the best. Did you know that regular hot dogs have as many as 15 grams of fat?

Dubuque's Extra-Lean Reduced-Sodium **ham** tastes wonderful, reduces the sodium as well as the fat, and gives you a larger serving. Don't be fooled by products called turkey ham; they may *not* be lower in fat than a very lean pork product. Here's one label as an example: I checked a brand of turkey ham called Genoa. It gives you a 2-ounce serving for 70 calories and 3½ grams of fat. The Dubuque extra-lean ham, made from pork, gives you a 3-ounce serving for 90 calories, but only 2½ grams of fat. *You get more food and less fat.*

The same can be true for packaged **ground turkey;** if you're not buying *fresh* ground turkey, you may be getting a product with turkey skin and a lot of fat ground up in it. Look to be sure the package is labeled with the fat content; if it isn't, run the other way!

Your best bets in **snack foods** are pretzels, which are always low in fat, as well as the chips from the Guiltless Gourmet, which taste especially good with one of my dips.

Frozen dinners can be expensive and high in sodium, but it's smart to have two or three in the freezer as a backup when your best-laid plans go awry and you need to grab something on the run. But it's not a good idea to rely on them too much—what if you can't get to the store to get them, or you're short on cash? The sodium can be high in some of them because they often replace the fat with salt, so do read the labels. Also ask yourself if the serving is enough to satisfy you; for many of us, it's not.

Egg substitute is expensive, and probably not necessary unless you're cooking for someone who has to worry about every bit of cholesterol in their diet. If you occasionally have a fried egg or an omelet, *use the real egg.* For cooking, you can usually substitute two egg whites for one whole egg. Most of the time it won't make any difference, but check your recipe carefully.

Frozen pizzas aren't particularly healthy, but used occasionally, in moderation, they're okay. Your best bet is to make your own using the Pillsbury French Crust. Take a look at the frozen pizza package of your choice, though, because you may find that plain cheese pizza, which you might think would be the healthiest, might actually have the most fat. Since there's nothing else on there, they have to cover the crust with a heavy layer of high-fat cheese. A veggie pizza generally uses less cheese and more healthy, crunchy vegetables.

Healthy frozen desserts are hard to find except for the Weight Watchers brands. I've always felt that their portions are so small, and for their size still pretty high in fat and sugar. (This is one of the reasons I think I'll be successful marketing my frozen desserts someday. After Cliff tasted one of my earliest healthy pies—and licked the plate clean—he remarked that if I ever opened a restaurant, people would keep coming back for my desserts alone!) Keep an eye out for fat-free or very low-fat frozen yogurt or sorbet products. Even Häagen-Dazs, which makes some of the highest fat content ice cream, now has a fat-free fruit sorbet pop out that's pretty good. I'm sure there will be more before too long.

You have to be realistic: what are you willing to do, and what are you *not* willing to do? Let's take bread, for example. Some people just have to have the real thing—rye bread with caraway seeds or a whole-wheat version with bits of bran in it.

I prefer to use reduced-calorie **bread** because I like a *real* sandwich. This way, I can have two slices of bread and it counts as only one bread/starch exchange.

Do you love **croutons?** Forget the ones from the grocery store—they're extremely high in fat. Instead, take reduced-calorie bread, toast it, give it a quick spray of I Can't Believe It's Not Butter! Spray, and let it dry a bit. Cut the bread in cubes. Then, for an extra-good flavor, put the pieces in a plastic bag with a couple of tablespoons of Kraft House Italian (a reduced-fat Parmesan/Romano cheese blend) and shake them up. You might be surprised just how good they are! Another product that's really good for a crouton—Corn Chex cereal. Sprinkle a few Chex on top of your salad, and I think you'll be pleasantly surprised. I've also found that Rice Chex, crushed up, with parsley flakes and a little bit of Parmesan cheese, makes a great topping for casseroles that you used to put potato chips on.

Salad toppers can make a lot of difference in how content you feel after you've eaten. Some low-fat cheese, some homemade croutons, and even some bacon bits on top of your greens deliver an abundance of tasty satisfaction. I always use the real Hormel **bacon bits** instead of the imitation bacon-flavored bits. I only use a small amount, but you get that real bacon flavor—and less fat too.

How I Shop for Myself

I always keep my kitchen stocked with my basic staples; that way, I can go to the cupboard and create new recipes any time I'm inspired. I hope you will take the time (and allot the money) to stock your cupboards with items from the staples list, so you can enjoy developing your own healthy versions of family favorites without making extra trips to the market.

I'm always on the lookout for new products sitting on the grocery shelf. When I spot something I haven't seen before, I'll usually grab it, glance at the front, then turn it around and read the label carefully. I call it looking at the promises (the "come-on" on the front of the package) and then at the warranty (the ingredients list and the label on the back).

If it looks as good on the back as it does on the front, I'll say okay and either create a recipe on the spot or take it home for when I do think of something to do with it. Picking up a new product is just about the only time I buy something not on my list.

The items on my shopping list are normal, everyday foods, but as low-fat and low-sugar (*while still tasting good*) as I can find. I can make any recipe in this book as long as these staples are on my shelves. After using these products for a couple of weeks, you will find it becomes routine to have them on hand. And I promise you, I really don't spend any more at the store now than I did a few years ago when I told myself I couldn't afford some of these items. Back then, of course, plenty of unhealthy, high-priced snacks I really didn't need somehow made the magic leap from the grocery shelves into my cart. Who was I kidding?

Yes, you often have to pay a little more for fat-free or low-fat products, including meats. But since I frequently use a half pound of meat to serve four to six people, your cost per serving will be much lower.

Try adding up what you were spending before on chips and cookies, premium brand ice cream and fatty cuts of meat, and you'll soon see that we've *streamlined* your shopping cart, and taken the weight off your pocketbook as well as your hips!

Remember, your good health is *your* business—but it's big business too. Write to the manufacturers of products you and your family enjoy but feel are just too high in fat, sugar, or sodium to be part of your new healthy lifestyle. Companies are spending millions of dollars to respond to consumers' concerns about food products, and I bet that in the next few years, you'll discover fat-free and low-fat versions of nearly every product piled high on your supermarket shelves!

The Healthy Exchanges Kitchen

You might be surprised to discover I still don't have a massive test kitchen stocked with every modern appliance and handy gadget ever made. The tiny galley kitchen where I first launched Healthy Exchanges has room for only one person at a time, but it never stopped me from feeling the sky's the limit when it comes to seeking out great healthy taste!

Because storage is at such a premium in my kitchen, I don't waste space with equipment I don't really need. Here's a list of what I consider worth having. If you notice serious gaps in your equipment, you can probably find most of what you need at a local discount store or garage sale. If your kitchen is equipped with more sophisticated appliances, don't feel guilty about using them. Enjoy every appliance you can find room for or that you can afford. Just be assured that healthy, quick, and delicious food can be prepared with the "basics."

A Healthy Exchanges Kitchen Equipment List

Good-quality nonstick skillets (medium, large)
Good-quality saucepans (small, medium, large)
Glass mixing bowls (small, medium, large)
Glass measures (1-cup, 2-cup, 4-cup, 8-cup)

Sharp knives (paring, chef, butcher)
Rubber spatulas
Wire whisks
Measuring spoons
Measuring cups
Large mixing spoons
Egg separator
Covered jar
Vegetable parer
Grater
Potato masher
Electric mixer
Electric blender
Electric skillet
4-inch round custard dishes
Glass pie plates
8-by-8-inch glass baking dishes
Cake pans (9-by-9, 9-by-13-inch)
10¾-by-7-by-1½-inch biscuit pan
Cookie sheets (good nonstick ones)
Jelly-roll pan
Muffin tins
5-by-9-inch bread pan
Plastic colander
Cutting board
Pie wedge server
Cooking timer
Slow cooker
Air popper for popcorn
Kitchen scales (unless you *always* use my recipes)
Wire racks for cooling baked goods
Electric toaster oven (to conserve energy for those times when
    only one item is being baked or for a recipe that requires a
    short baking time)
Square-shaped server
Can opener (I prefer manual)
Rolling pin

How to Read a Healthy Exchanges Recipe

The Healthy Exchanges Nutritional Analysis

Before using these recipes you may wish to consult your physician or health-care provider to be sure they are appropriate for you. The information in this book is not intended to take the place of any medical advice. It reflects my experiences, studies, research, and opinions regarding healthy eating.

Each recipe includes nutritional information calculated in three ways:

> Healthy Exchanges Weight Loss Choices™ or Exchanges
> Calories, fiber, and fat grams
> Diabetic exchanges

In every Healthy Exchanges recipe, the diabetic exchanges have been calculated by a Registered Dietitian. All the other calculations were done by computer, using the Food Processor II software. When the ingredient listing gives more than one choice, the first ingredient listed is the one used in the recipe analysis. Due to inevitable variations in the ingredients you choose to use, the nutritional values should be considered approximate.

The annotation "(limited)" following Protein counts in some

recipes indicates that consumption of whole eggs should be limited to four per week.

Please note the following symbols:

☆This star means read the recipe's directions carefully for special instructions about **division** of ingredients.

❋ This symbol indicates **FREEZES WELL**.

A Few Cooking

Terms to Ease the

Way

Everyone can learn to cook *The Healthy Exchanges Way*. It's simple, it's quick, and the results are delicious! If you've tended to avoid the kitchen because you find recipe instructions confusing or complicated, I hope I can help you feel more confident. I'm not offering a full cooking course here, just some terms I use often that I know you'll want to understand.

Bake: To cook food in the oven; sometimes called roasting

Beat: To mix very fast with a spoon, wire whisk, or electric mixer

Blend: To mix two or more ingredients together thoroughly so that the mixture is smooth

Boil: To cook in liquid until bubbles form

Brown: To cook at low to medium-low heat until ingredients turn brown

Chop: To cut food into small pieces with a knife, blender, or food processor

Combine: To mix ingredients together with a spoon

Cool: To let stand at room temperature until food is no longer hot to the touch

Dice: To chop into small, even-sized pieces

Drain: To pour off liquid; sometimes you will need to reserve the liquid to use in the recipe, so please read carefully.

Drizzle:	To sprinkle drops of liquid (for example, chocolate syrup) lightly over top of food
Fold in:	To combine delicate ingredients with other foods by using a gentle, circular motion. Example: adding Cool Whip Lite to an already stirred-up bowl of pudding.
Preheat:	To heat your oven to the desired temperature, usually about 10 minutes before you put your food in to bake
Sauté:	To cook in skillet or frying pan until food is soft
Simmer:	To cook in a small amount of liquid over low heat; this lets the flavors blend without too much liquid evaporating.
Whisk:	To beat with a wire whisk until mixture is well mixed; don't worry about finesse here, just use some elbow grease!

How to Measure

I try to make it as easy as possible by providing more than one measurement for many ingredients in my recipes—both the weight in ounces and the amount measured by a measuring cup, for example. Just remember:

- You measure **solids** (flour, Cool Whip Lite, yogurt, macaroni, nonfat dry milk powder) in your set of separate measuring cups (¼, ⅓, ½, 1 cup)

- You measure **liquids** (Diet Mountain Dew, water, tomato juice) in the clear glass or plastic measuring cups that measure ounces, cups, and pints. Set the cup on a level surface and pour the liquid into it, or you may get too much.

- You can use your measuring spoon set for liquids or solids. **Note:** Don't pour a liquid like an extract into a measuring spoon held over the bowl in case you overpour; instead, do it over the sink.

Here are a few handy equivalents:

3 teaspoons	equals	1 tablespoon
4 tablespoons	equals	¼ cup
5⅓ tablespoons	equals	⅓ cup
8 tablespoons	equals	½ cup
10⅔ tablespoons	equals	⅔ cup
12 tablespoons	equals	¾ cup
16 tablespoons	equals	1 cup
2 cups	equals	1 pint
4 cups	equals	1 quart
8 ounces liquid	equals	1 fluid cup

That's it. Now, ready, set, cook!

Soups

It warms the heart and fills the tummy, but for the frugal chef, soup is also a wonderful way to use up leftovers! Half an onion sitting on a shelf? Chop it up and toss it in! A chunk of chicken that looks too small to feed your family of four? Not when it's diced and combined with other tasty ingredients in my Chunky Chicken Soup. And when you're cooking up noodles or pasta for a main dish sometime, add some extra to the pot—and you've got the beginnings of a pot of soup.

Soups

Cream of Mushroom Soup

Why would I create a recipe for this most beloved cream soup of all when you can already find it in a can? Well, my Healthy Exchanges version boasts more fresh mushrooms and a special blend of spices, but my best reason is a simple one: I think this is just the creamiest healthy soup I've ever tried! ☺ Serves 4 (1 cup)

2 cups chopped fresh mushrooms
½ cup chopped onion
½ teaspoon dried minced garlic
2 cups (one 16-ounce can) Healthy Request Chicken Broth
1 tablespoon reduced-sodium soy sauce
¼ teaspoon black pepper
1½ cups (one 12-fluid-ounce can) Carnation Evaporated Skim
    Milk
6 tablespoons all-purpose flour

In a large saucepan sprayed with butter-flavored cooking spray, sauté mushrooms, onion, and garlic for 5 minutes or until mushrooms start to turn limp. Add chicken broth. Mix well to combine. Bring mixture to a boil. Lower heat. Stir in soy sauce and black pepper. In a covered jar, combine evaporated skim milk and flour. Shake well to blend. Pour milk mixture into mushroom mixture. Continue simmering until mixture thickens, stirring often.

Each serving equals:

HE: 1¼ Vegetable • ¾ Skim Milk • ½ Bread •
8 Optional Calories

156 Calories • 0 gm Fat • 12 gm Protein •
27 gm Carbohydrate • 808 mg Sodium •
293 mg Calcium • 3 gm Fiber

DIABETIC: 1 Skim Milk • 1 Starch • ½ Vegetable

Cream of Tomato Soup

For those times when you don't feel like a heavy meal, soup makes terrifically nourishing and soothing lighter fare! You'll be astonished at how rich this homemade version of your childhood favorite tastes—and how simple it can be to fix it!

○ Serves 4 (1½ cups)

> 3 cups (one 28-ounce can) tomatoes, coarsely chopped and
>   undrained
> ½ cup chopped onion
> ½ cup chopped celery
> ¼ cup chopped fresh parsley
> 3 cups skim milk
> ¼ cup all-purpose flour
> 1 teaspoon dried parsley flakes
> ⅛ teaspoon black pepper

In a large covered saucepan, combine undrained tomatoes, onion, celery, and fresh parsley. Cook over medium-low heat for 10 minutes or until vegetables are tender. Pour hot mixture into a blender container. Cover and process on BLEND for 30 seconds or until smooth. In a large covered jar, combine skim milk and flour. Shake well to blend. Pour milk mixture into a large saucepan sprayed with butter-flavored cooking spray. Cook over medium heat until mixture starts to thicken, stirring constantly. Add blended tomato mixture, parsley flakes, and black pepper. Mix well to combine. Lower heat and simmer for 10 minutes or until mixture is heated through.

Each serving equals:

HE: 2 Vegetable • ¾ Skim Milk • ⅓ Bread

141 Calories • 1 gm Fat • 9 gm Protein •
24 gm Carbohydrate • 127 mg Sodium •
265 mg Calcium • 3 gm Fiber

DIABETIC: 2 Vegetable • 1 Skim Milk

Cream of Potato and Cabbage Soup

Hearty soups are a wonderful way to feed your family without spending a lot, but they won't notice your smart economy, just the cozy feeling that a big bowl of soup always delivers! If your kids love mashed potatoes as much as mine do, they'll look forward with glee to supper when it features this thick and appetizing creamy soup.

◐ Serves 4 (1¼ cups)

2 cups (one 16-ounce can) Healthy Request Chicken Broth

¼ teaspoon dried minced garlic

½ cup sliced green onion with tops

1 cup shredded carrots

2 cups shredded cabbage

1½ cups (one 12-fluid-ounce can) Carnation Evaporated Skim Milk

1 cup skim milk

1⅓ cups (3 ounces) instant potato flakes

¼ teaspoon black pepper

1 teaspoon dried parsley flakes

In a medium saucepan, combine chicken broth and garlic. Add onion, carrots, and cabbage. Mix well to combine. Cook over medium heat for 10 minutes or until vegetables are tender. Add evaporated skim milk, skim milk, potato flakes, black pepper, and parsley flakes. Mix well to combine. Lower heat and simmer for 5 minutes, or until mixture thickens and is heated through, stirring often.

Each serving equals:

HE: 1¾ Vegetable • 1 Skim Milk • 1 Bread • 8 Optional Calories

184 Calories • 0 gm Fat • 13 gm Protein • 33 gm Carbohydrate • 420 mg Sodium • 390 mg Calcium • 3 gm Fiber

DIABETIC: 1 Vegetable • 1 Skim Milk • 1 Starch

Italian Bean Soup

Maybe it's because their gardens produce such glorious produce, but there's a long tradition of main-dish soups in the Mediterranean countries, especially Italy. When you top a steaming bowl of beans and veggies with just a touch of fragrant Parmesan cheese, you've turned an ordinary meal into a banquet for the taste buds!

● Serves 4 (1½ cups)

½ cup chopped onion

2 cups (one 16-ounce can) tomatoes, coarsely chopped and undrained

10 ounces (one 16-ounce can) great northern beans, rinsed and drained

½ cup (one 2.5-ounce jar) sliced mushrooms, drained

2 cups (one 16-ounce can) cut green beans, rinsed and drained

1 (10¾-ounce) can Healthy Request Tomato Soup

½ cup water

1 teaspoon Italian seasoning

1 teaspoon Sugar Twin or Sprinkle Sweet

¼ cup (¾ ounce) grated Kraft fat-free Parmesan cheese

In a large saucepan sprayed with butter-flavored cooking spray, sauté onion for 5 minutes or just until tender. Meanwhile, place undrained tomatoes in a blender container, cover, and process on BLEND for 15 seconds or until smooth. Stir blended tomatoes into skillet with onion. Add great northern beans, mushrooms, green beans, tomato soup, water, Italian seasoning, and Sugar Twin. Mix well to combine. Bring mixture to a boil. Lower heat and simmer for 10 minutes, stirring occasionally. When serving, sprinkle 1 tablespoon Parmesan cheese over top of each bowl.

Each serving equals:

HE: 2½ Vegetable • 1½ Protein • ½ Slider •
6 Optional Calories

197 Calories • 1 gm Fat • 9 gm Protein •
38 gm Carbohydrate • 437 mg Sodium •
84 mg Calcium • 8 gm Fiber

DIABETIC: 2 Vegetable • 1½ Starch • 1 Meat

Peasant Vegetable Bean Soup

Even if you make your home in one of our big cities, there's no reason not to "live off the land" . . . just "harvest" your ingredients at the weekly farmers' market! The peasant tradition has always celebrated the ripest and best from the fields, and this soup will make your family smack their lips in delight.

○ Serves 6 (1⅓ cups)

> 4 cups (two 16-ounce cans) tomatoes, coarsely chopped and
>   undrained
> 2 cups water
> ½ cup finely chopped celery
> ½ cup chopped onion
> 2 cups shredded cabbage
> 2 teaspoons chili seasoning
> ⅛ teaspoon black pepper
> 1 teaspoon dried parsley flakes
> 10 ounces (one 16-ounce can) pinto beans, rinsed and drained
> 10 ounces (one 16-ounce can) red kidney beans, rinsed and drained

Place undrained tomatoes in a blender container. Cover and process on BLEND for 15 seconds or until smooth. Pour blended tomatoes into a large saucepan. Add water, celery, onion, cabbage, chili seasoning, black pepper, and parsley flakes. Mix well to combine. Stir in pinto beans and kidney beans. Bring mixture to a boil. Lower heat and simmer for 30 minutes, stirring occasionally.

Each serving equals:

HE: 2⅓ Vegetable • 1⅔ Protein

---

148 Calories • 0 gm Fat • 8 gm Protein •
29 gm Carbohydrate • 276 mg Sodium •
95 mg Calcium • 9 gm Fiber

DIABETIC: 1½ Vegetable • 1 Starch • 1 Meat

Heartland Beef and Noodle Soup ❄

So many of our smartest, thriftiest recipes have come from the Midwest, most of them created by farm wives who often had to make do with less than they'd like! My own mother worked magic in the kitchen with leftover bits of this and that, instilling in me a desire to be just such a creative cook. This flavorful soup is a good example of doing a lot with just a little! ☯ Serves 4 (1½ cups)

> 1 full cup (6 ounces) diced cooked lean roast beef
> ½ cup chopped onion
> 1¾ cups (one 14½-ounce can) Swanson Beef Broth
> 2¼ cups water
> ⅛ teaspoon black pepper
> ¼ teaspoon dried minced garlic
> 1¾ cups (3 ounces) uncooked noodles
> ½ cup (one 2.5-ounce jar) sliced mushrooms, drained
> 1 teaspoon dried parsley flakes

In a large saucepan sprayed with butter-flavored cooking spray, sauté roast beef and onion for 5 minutes or until onion is tender. Add beef broth, water, black pepper, and garlic. Mix well to combine. Bring mixture to a boil. Lower heat and simmer for 10 minutes. Stir in uncooked noodles, mushrooms, and parsley flakes. Cover and continue simmering for 10 minutes or until noodles are tender, stirring occasionally.

HINT: If you don't have leftovers, purchase a chunk of cooked lean roast beef from your local deli.

Each serving equals:

HE: 1½ Protein • 1 Bread • ½ Vegetable •
8 Optional Calories

---

188 Calories • 4 gm Fat • 17 gm Protein •
21 gm Carbohydrate • 475 mg Sodium •
19 mg Calcium • 2 gm Fiber

DIABETIC: 1½ Meat • 1½ Starch/Carbohydrate

Chunky Chicken Soup

Here's a great example of how economizing on meat doesn't have to mean feeling deprived! By boosting the flavor content of this rich soup with so many tasty veggies, I can make six ounces of chicken feed a family of four—and nobody leaves the table hungry.

◐ Serves 4 (1½ cups)

½ cup chopped onion
½ cup chopped green bell pepper
1 cup sliced celery
½ teaspoon dried minced garlic
1¾ cups (one 15-ounce can) Hunt's Chunky Tomato Sauce
2 cups (one 16-ounce can) Healthy Request Chicken Broth
1 full cup (6 ounces) diced cooked chicken breast
1 cup water
⅔ cup (2 ounces) uncooked Minute Rice
1 cup fresh or frozen whole-kernel corn
1 cup fresh or frozen cut green beans or okra
½ teaspoon Tabasco sauce
1 tablespoon Creole seasoning
⅛ teaspoon black pepper

In a large saucepan sprayed with butter-flavored cooking spray, sauté onion, green pepper, and celery for 10 minutes or until tender. Add garlic, tomato sauce, chicken broth, chicken, and water. Mix well to combine. Stir in uncooked rice, corn, and green beans. Add Tabasco sauce, Creole seasoning, and black pepper. Mix well to combine. Bring mixture to a boil. Lower heat and simmer for 25 to 30 minutes, stirring occasionally.

HINT: If you don't have leftovers, purchase a chunk of cooked chicken breast from your local deli.

Each serving equals:

HE: 3¼ Vegetable • 1½ Protein • 1 Bread •
8 Optional Calories

---

194 Calories • 2 gm Fat • 18 gm Protein •
26 gm Carbohydrate • 1,002 mg Sodium •
36 mg Calcium • 4 gm Fiber

DIABETIC: 3 Vegetable • 1½ Meat • 1 Starch

Tex-Mex Vegetable Soup

This spicy down-home veggie soup could almost be called a chili, it's so jam-packed with mouthwatering ingredients! Besides delivering a lot of nutrition and flavor, it's easily prepared in little more than a half hour. And it's so filling, it's perfect for satisfying a tableful of hungry kids! ☻ Serves 6 (1½ cups)

> 16 ounces ground 90% lean turkey or beef
> 1 cup chopped onion
> 1 cup chopped celery
> 1¾ cups (one 14½-ounce can) Swanson Beef Broth
> 2 cups Healthy Request tomato juice or any reduced-sodium
>   tomato juice
> 6 ounces (one 8-ounce can) red kidney beans, rinsed and drained
> 2 cups (one 16-ounce can) tomatoes, coarsely chopped and
>   undrained
> 1½ cups frozen whole-kernel corn
> 1 cup frozen sliced carrots
> 1 cup frozen cut green beans
> ½ teaspoon dried minced garlic
> 2 teaspoons chili seasoning
> ¼ teaspoon black pepper

In a large saucepan sprayed with olive oil–flavored cooking spray, brown meat and onion. Add celery, beef broth, tomato juice, kidney beans, undrained tomatoes, corn, carrots, and green beans. Mix well to combine. Stir in garlic, chili seasoning, and black pepper. Bring mixture to a boil. Lower heat, cover, and simmer for 30 minutes, stirring occasionally.

Each serving equals:

HE: 2⅔ Vegetable • 2½ Protein • ½ Bread •
6 Optional Calories

235 Calories • 7 gm Fat • 19 gm Protein •
24 gm Carbohydrate • 394 mg Sodium •
42 mg Calcium • 5 gm Fiber

DIABETIC: 2 Vegetable • 2 Meat • 1 Starch

Ham and Corn Chowder

Cliff loves a thick corn chowder, especially when it's chock-full of potatoes and little bits of ham like this one. When you can make something so delicious and satisfying so quickly, you'll never have to worry about what to serve for supper.

© Serves 4 (1½ cups)

> 1¼ cups water
> 1 cup (5 ounces) diced raw potatoes
> ½ cup chopped onion
> 1 full cup (6 ounces) diced Dubuque 97% fat-free ham or any
>   extra-lean ham
> 2 cups (one 16-ounce can) cream-style corn
> 1 cup skim milk
> 1 (10¾-ounce) can Healthy Request Cream of Mushroom Soup
> 1 teaspoon dried parsley flakes
> ¼ teaspoon black pepper

In a medium saucepan, combine water, potatoes, and onion. Cook over medium heat until potatoes are just tender. Stir in ham, corn, skim milk, mushroom soup, parsley flakes, and black pepper. Lower heat and simmer for 15 minutes, stirring occasionally.

Each serving equals:

HE: 1¼ Bread • 1 Protein • ¼ Skim Milk •
¼ Vegetable • ½ Slider • 1 Optional Calorie

231 Calories • 3 gm Fat • 12 gm Protein •
39 gm Carbohydrate • 1,059 mg Sodium •
138 mg Calcium • 2 gm Fiber

DIABETIC: 2½ Starch/Carbohydrate • 1 Meat

Chunky Bean and Franks Soup

Tired of serving hot dogs the same old way, but can't seem to think of what else to do with this economical source of healthy protein? Why not stir up this fragrant and robust combination, then just enjoy the oohs and aahs of your family as they gobble it down?

Serves 4 (1½ cups)

> 8 ounces Healthy Choice 97% fat-free frankfurters, diced
> 10 ounces (one 16-ounce can) great northern beans, rinsed and drained
> 2 cups (one 16-ounce can) French-style green beans, rinsed and drained
> 1 (10¾-ounce) can Healthy Request Tomato Soup
> 1¾ cups (one 14½-ounce can) Swanson Beef Broth
> ¼ teaspoon black pepper

In a medium saucepan, combine frankfurters, great northern beans, green beans, and tomato soup. Add beef broth and black pepper. Mix well to combine. Bring mixture to a boil. Lower heat and simmer for 15 minutes, stirring occasionally.

Each serving equals:

HE: 2½ Protein • 1 Vegetable • ½ Slider • 13 Optional Calories

---

219 Calories • 3 gm Fat • 16 gm Protein • 32 gm Carbohydrate • 1,166 mg Sodium • 74 mg Calcium • 5 gm Fiber

---

DIABETIC: 2 Meat • 1½ Starch • 1 Vegetable

Main Dish Salads

Any restaurant chef will tell you, it's all in the presentation—and this section provides lots of ideas for stretching a modest amount of fish or meat into a delicious and satisfying entree! If you've got just a cup of diced chicken breast, a family of four will dine like conquistadors when you serve Chicken Mexicali Pasta Salad. And just a few ounces more turns a chunk of ham into a star when Roman Carrot and Ham Pasta Salad is on the menu!

Main Dish Salads

Vegetable-Bean Pasta Salad

Too hot to turn on the oven, but you've got a houseful of ravenous kids to feed? Here's a delectable pasta salad that will fill up everyone's tummies—but not fill out your hips! This features one of my favorite tangy dressings, and I hope you'll agree it's a dish to be savored again and again.   ☻   Serves 8 (¾ cup)

> 2 cups cold cooked rotini pasta, rinsed and drained
> 10 ounces (one 16-ounce can) red kidney beans, rinsed and
>   drained
> ¼ cup chopped onion
> ¼ cup chopped green bell pepper
> 2 cups (one 16-ounce can) cut green beans, rinsed and drained
> 1 tablespoon + 1 teaspoon all-purpose flour
> 1½ teaspoons lemon pepper
> ½ cup white vinegar
> ½ cup Sugar Twin or Sprinkle Sweet
> ⅓ cup water
> 4 teaspoons reduced-calorie margarine
> 1 tablespoon prepared mustard

In a large bowl, combine rotini pasta, kidney beans, onion, green pepper, and green beans. In a covered jar, combine flour, lemon pepper, vinegar, Sugar Twin, and water. Shake well to blend. Pour mixture into a medium saucepan sprayed with butter-flavored cooking spray. Add margarine and mustard. Mix well to combine. Cook over medium heat until mixture thickens, stirring constantly. Place saucepan on a wire rack and let set for 5 minutes. Stir sauce mixture into pasta mixture. Cover and refrigerate for at least 30 minutes. Gently stir again just before serving.

HINT: 1½ cups uncooked rotini pasta usually cooks to about 2
    cups.

Each serving equals:

HE: ⅔ Protein • ⅔ Vegetable • ½ Bread • ¼ Fat •
11 Optional Calories

105 Calories • 1 gm Fat • 4 gm Protein •
20 gm Carbohydrate • 169 mg Sodium •
24 mg Calcium • 3 gm Fiber

DIABETIC: 1 Vegetable • 1 Starch

Dijon Tuna Macaroni Salad

If you picked up a half dozen cans of tuna on sale, but you're tired of tuna casserole and tuna sandwiches, here's a fresh and fun way to stir up a little lunchtime excitement at your house! Yes, a jar of "gourmet" mustard may cost a little more, but a little of it goes such a long way toward making your meals extra-special!

◐   Serves 4 (1 full cup)

> 1½ cups cold cooked elbow macaroni, rinsed and drained
> ½ cup frozen peas, thawed
> ¾ cup finely diced celery
> ¼ cup finely chopped onion
> ½ cup Kraft fat-free mayonnaise
> 1 tablespoon white vinegar
> Sugar substitute to equal 1 tablespoon sugar
> 1 tablespoon Grey Poupon Country Dijon Mustard
> ¼ teaspoon black pepper
> 1 teaspoon dried parsley flakes
> 2 (6-ounce) cans white tuna, packed in water, drained and flaked
> 1 hard-boiled egg, finely chopped

In a large bowl, combine macaroni, peas, celery, and onion. In a small bowl, combine mayonnaise, vinegar, sugar substitute, mustard, black pepper, and parsley flakes. Add mayonnaise mixture to macaroni mixture. Mix well to combine. Stir in tuna and egg. Cover and refrigerate for at least 30 minutes. Gently stir again just before serving.

HINTS: 1. 1 cup uncooked macaroni usually cooks to about 1½ cups.

2. Thaw peas by placing in a colander and rinsing under hot water for one minute.

3. If you want the look and feel of egg without the cholesterol, toss out the yolk and dice the whites.

Each serving equals:

HE: 1¾ Protein • 1 Bread • ½ Vegetable • ¼ Slider • 2 Optional Calories

235 Calories • 3 gm Fat • 27 gm Protein • 25 gm Carbohydrate • 675 mg Sodium • 37 mg Calcium • 2 gm Fiber

DIABETIC: 3 Meat • 1½ Starch

Oriental Tuna and Green Bean Salad

There's something irresistible about a crunchy salad, and this one is about the crunchiest you'll ever meet! The dressing perks up your taste buds, and the almonds give this succulent blend a little added pizzazz. Do as the great Asian chefs do—slice your celery on a slant to make it prettier and tastier. ☻ Serves 6 (¾ cup)

> 3 cups frozen French-style green beans
> 1½ cups water
> ½ cup Kraft fat-free mayonnaise
> 1 tablespoon lemon juice
> 1½ tablespoons reduced-sodium soy sauce
> ¼ teaspoon dried minced garlic
> 1 (6-ounce) can white tuna, packed in water, drained and flaked
> 1 cup thinly sliced celery
> 2 tablespoons (½ ounce) slivered almonds
> 1 cup (2¼ ounces) coarsely chopped chow mein noodles

In a medium saucepan, cook beans in water just until tender. Drain well and cool. In a large bowl, combine mayonnaise, lemon juice, soy sauce, and garlic. Add green beans, tuna, and celery. Mix gently to combine. Cover and refrigerate for at least 30 minutes. Just before serving, stir in almonds and chow mein noodles.

Each serving equals:

HE: 1⅓ Vegetable • ½ Protein • ½ Bread • ¼ Slider • 5 Optional Calories

128 Calories • 4 gm Fat • 10 gm Protein • 13 gm Carbohydrate • 447 mg Sodium • 38 mg Calcium • 2 gm Fiber

DIABETIC: 1 Vegetable • 1 Meat • ½ Fat • ½ Starch/Carbohydrate

Chicken Mexicali Pasta Salad

Here's a truly festive mix of flavors and textures that's bound to elicit an "Olé" or two around your table! Go as hot as you dare with the salsa, but first be sure that everyone at the table enjoys steam coming out of their ears the way Cliff does!   ◐   Serves 4 (¾ cup)

> 1 full cup (6 ounces) diced cooked chicken breast
> ⅓ cup Kraft fat-free mayonnaise
> ½ cup chunky salsa (mild, medium, or hot)
> ¼ teaspoon dried minced garlic
> 1 teaspoon dried parsley flakes
> 1½ cups cold cooked rotini pasta, rinsed and drained
> ½ cup frozen whole-kernel corn, thawed

In a medium bowl, combine chicken, mayonnaise, salsa, garlic, and parsley flakes. Add rotini pasta and corn. Mix gently to combine. Cover and refrigerate for at least 30 minutes. Gently stir again just before serving.

HINTS: 1. If you don't have leftovers, purchase a chunk of cooked chicken breast from your local deli.

2. 1 cup uncooked rotini pasta usually cooks to about 1½ cups.

3. Thaw corn by placing in a colander and rinsing under hot water for one minute.

Each serving equals:

HE: 1½ Protein • 1 Bread • ¼ Vegetable •
13 Optional Calories

---

201 Calories • 1 gm Fat • 16 gm Protein •
23 gm Carbohydrate • 315 mg Sodium •
52 mg Calcium • 1 gm Fiber

DIABETIC: 1½ Meat • 1½ Starch • ½ Vegetable

BBQ Chicken and Macaroni Salad

If you're struggling to make ends meet, must you go to the extra expense of buying healthy versions of popular products like barbecue sauce? Here's my philosophy: first, a little goes a long way toward making your healthy recipe extra-yummy, and second, spending a little more to ensure good health always saves you money—if not now, then later on!　　◐　　Serves 6 (⅔ cup)

> 2 cups cold cooked elbow macaroni, rinsed and drained
> 1 cup frozen peas, thawed
> 1 full cup (6 ounces) diced cooked chicken breast
> ½ cup Kraft fat-free mayonnaise
> 3 tablespoons Healthy Choice BBQ sauce
> 1 teaspoon dried parsley flakes

In a large bowl, combine macaroni, peas, and chicken. In a small bowl, combine mayonnaise, BBQ sauce, and parsley flakes. Add mayonnaise mixture to macaroni mixture. Mix gently to combine. Cover and refrigerate for at least 30 minutes. Gently stir again just before serving.

HINTS: 1. 1⅓ cups uncooked elbow macaroni usually cooks to about 2 cups.

2. Thaw peas by placing in a colander and rinsing under hot water for one minute.

3. If you don't have leftovers, purchase a chunk of cooked chicken breast from your local deli.

Each serving equals:

HE: 1 Bread • 1 Protein • ¼ Slider • 1 Optional Calorie

142 Calories • 1 gm Fat • 12 gm Protein • 21 gm Carbohydrate • 260 mg Sodium • 15 mg Calcium • 2 gm Fiber

DIABETIC: 1½ Starch/Carbohydrate • 1 Meat

Chunky Chicken Club Salad

That wonderful all-American lunch tradition known as the club sandwich is very high in calories and fat when prepared in classic style. Why not enjoy all those scrumptious flavors in an easy-to-fix main-dish salad, and join the "club" devoted to a lifetime of good health?　　❍　　Serves 4 (2 cups)

> 1 full cup (6 ounces) diced Dubuque 97% fat-free ham or any
> 　　extra-lean ham
> 1 full cup (6 ounces) diced cooked chicken breast
> ⅓ cup Kraft Fat Free French Dressing
> ¼ cup chopped onion
> ½ cup chopped celery
> 2 tablespoons Hormel Bacon Bits
> 2¾ cups finely shredded lettuce
> 1 cup chopped fresh tomato
> 2 slices reduced-calorie bread, toasted and cubed

In a large bowl, combine ham, chicken, French dressing, onion, celery, and bacon bits. Just before serving, add lettuce, tomato, and toast cubes. Toss gently to combine.

HINT:　If you don't have leftovers, purchase a chunk of cooked chicken breast from your local deli.

Each serving equals:

> HE: 2½ Bread • 2¼ Vegetable • ¼ Bread •
> ½ Slider • 6 Optional Calories
> _____
> 204 Calories • 4 gm Fat • 24 gm Protein •
> 18 gm Carbohydrate • 793 mg Sodium •
> 33 mg Calcium • 3 gm Fiber
> _____
> DIABETIC: 2½ Meat • 1 Vegetable • ½ Starch

Roman Carrot and Ham Pasta Salad

Budget meals don't have to look or taste as if you're scrimping, as long as you toss together such crunchy and colorful ingredients as this inviting salad does! Can't you just imagine sitting in a cafe in the Eternal City and nibbling on this delight as you gaze at its beautiful sights? (If you can't afford a plane ticket, stir this up for lunch and borrow a video of Italy from the library!)　　❂　　Serves 6 (1 cup)

> 2 cups (one 16-ounce can) sliced carrots, rinsed and drained
> ½ cup chopped onion
> ½ cup chopped green bell pepper
> 1 (10¾-ounce) can Healthy Request Tomato Soup
> 2 tablespoons Sugar Twin or Sprinkle Sweet
> ½ cup Kraft Fat Free Italian Dressing
> 2 tablespoons cider vinegar
> 2 teaspoons prepared mustard
> 2 teaspoons Worcestershire sauce
> 1½ cups (9 ounces) diced Dubuque 97% fat-free ham or any
>   extra-lean ham
> 2 cups cold cooked rotini pasta, rinsed and drained

In a medium bowl, combine carrots, onion, and green pepper. In a small saucepan, combine tomato soup, Sugar Twin, Italian dressing, vinegar, mustard, and Worcestershire sauce. Bring mixture to a boil. Remove from heat. Pour hot mixture over carrot mixture. Mix gently to combine. Cover and refrigerate for at least 30 minutes. Stir in ham and rotini pasta. Re-cover and refrigerate for at least 30 minutes. Gently stir again just before serving.

HINT:　1 cup uncooked rotini pasta usually cooks to about 1½ cups.

Each serving equals:

HE: 1 Protein • 1 Vegetable • ⅔ Bread • ½ Slider • 3 Optional Calories

126 Calories • 2 gm Fat • 7 gm Protein • 20 gm Carbohydrate • 586 mg Sodium • 21 mg Calcium • 1 gm Fiber

DIABETIC: 1 Meat • 1 Starch/Carbohydrate • ½ Vegetable

Summertime Ham Pasta Salad

I find myself serving main-dish salads often during July and August, usually because the sunny days create an appetite for food that is inviting and light. This delicious blend is sure to become a family favorite at your house as it has at ours! ☻ Serves 4 (1 full cup)

> 1½ cups cold cooked rotini pasta, rinsed and drained
> 1 full cup (6 ounces) Dubuque 97% fat-free ham or any extra-lean ham
> 2 cups (one 16-ounce can) cut green beans, rinsed and drained
> 2 tablespoons dill pickle relish
> 1 teaspoon dried parsley flakes
> 1 teaspoon prepared mustard
> ¼ teaspoon black pepper
> ⅓ cup Kraft fat-free mayonnaise
> 1 hard-boiled egg, chopped

In a medium bowl, combine rotini pasta, ham, and green beans. In a small bowl, combine dill pickle relish, parsley flakes, mustard, black pepper, and mayonnaise. Add dressing mixture to pasta mixture. Mix gently to combine. Fold in egg. Cover and refrigerate for at least 30 minutes. Gently stir again just before serving.

HINTS:　1. 1 cup uncooked rotini pasta usually cooks to about 1½ cups.

2. If you want the look and feel of egg without the cholesterol, toss out the yolk and dice the whites.

Each serving equals:

HE: 1¼ Protein (¼ limited) • 1 Vegetable • ¾ Bread • 10 Optional Calories

183 Calories • 3 gm Fat • 12 gm Protein • 27 gm Carbohydrate • 633 mg Sodium • 34 mg Calcium • 2 gm Fiber

DIABETIC: 1½ Starch • 1 Vegetable • 1 Meat

Italian Chef's Salad

Why do they always call this entree salad the "chef's" salad? you may wonder. Probably because the first chef who served it was tidying up his larder and decided to toss in a bit of this and the last little piece of that, creating the delectable tradition that blends meat and cheese with assorted veggies. *Delicioso!*

◐ Serves 2

3 cups finely shredded lettuce
⅓ cup (1½ ounces) shredded Kraft reduced-fat mozzarella cheese
½ cup (3 ounces) finely diced Dubuque 97% fat-free ham or any
  extra-lean ham
¼ cup diced green bell pepper
¼ cup diced onion
½ cup sliced celery
1 cup diced fresh tomato
2 tablespoons (½ ounce) sliced ripe olives
¼ cup Kraft Fat Free Italian Dressing
1 hard-boiled egg, sliced

In a medium bowl, combine lettuce, mozzarella cheese, ham, green pepper, onion, celery, tomato, olives, and Italian dressing. Evenly divide onto 2 serving plates and garnish each with half the sliced egg.

Each serving equals:

HE: 2½ Protein (½ limited) • 5 Vegetable • ¼ Fat •
16 Optional Calories

196 Calories • 8 gm Fat • 18 gm Protein •
13 gm Carbohydrate • 842 mg Sodium •
192 mg Calcium • 2 gm Fiber

DIABETIC: 3 Vegetable • 2 Meat • ½ Fat

Creamy Italian Pasta Salad

If it's been a while since your husband or kids smacked their lips over lunch, why not wake them up with this flavorful blend that's almost as irresistible as a vacation on the Isle of Capri? A little pastrami goes a long way because it's such a rich-tasting meat, and the olives give it that extra taste of the Mediterranean.

● Serves 6 (1 cup)

> 3 cups cold cooked rotini pasta, rinsed and drained
> 2 (2.5-ounce) packages Carl Buddig 90% lean pastrami, diced
> ¾ cup (3 ounces) shredded Kraft reduced-fat mozzarella cheese
> ⅓ cup (1½ ounces) sliced ripe olives
> ⅓ cup Kraft Fat Free Italian Dressing
> ¼ cup Kraft fat-free mayonnaise
> ⅛ teaspoon black pepper

In a large bowl combine pasta, pastrami, mozzarella cheese, and olives. In a small bowl combine Italian dressing, mayonnaise, and black pepper. Add dressing mixture to pasta mixture. Mix gently to combine. Cover and refrigerate for at least 30 minutes. Gently stir again just before serving.

HINT: 2¼ cups uncooked rotini pasta usually cooks to about 3 cups.

Each serving equals:

HE: 1½ Protein • 1 Bread • ¼ Fat • 14 Optional Calories

185 Calories • 5 gm Fat • 12 gm Protein • 23 gm Carbohydrate • 628 mg Sodium • 103 mg Calcium • 1 gm Fiber

DIABETIC: 1½ Starch • 1 Meat • 1 Fat

Meatless Main Dishes

Even dyed-in-the-wool meat lovers will be surprised—and satisfied—how much they will enjoy a meal now and then without a bit of meat! There's so much other "talent" in these imaginative entrees, from the three fantastic cheeses in Garden Macaroni and Cheese Skillet to an abundance of mashed potatoes in Cabbage and Potato Patties. With these dishes, "less" is definitely more!

Meatless Main Dishes

Broccoli Rice Quiche

If you've ever made a traditional quiche, you know it's not only full of pricey ingredients but also high in fat and cholesterol. But now you can enjoy the special flavors of this French import without any guilt, just pure culinary pleasure. The rice crust is unusual, but you'll find it's unusually good. It's so luscious and golden-brown as it emerges from the oven, your taste buds will go into overdrive!

☻ Serves 6

> 2 cups hot cooked rice
> ¾ cup (3 ounces) grated Kraft reduced-fat Cheddar cheese☆
> 4 eggs, beaten, or equivalent in egg substitute☆
> 1½ cups frozen chopped broccoli, thawed
> ½ cup (one 2.5-ounce jar) sliced mushrooms, drained
> ½ cup chopped onion
> 1 teaspoon lemon pepper

Preheat oven to 375 degrees. Spray a 9-inch pie plate with butter-flavored cooking spray. In a large bowl, combine rice, ½ cup Cheddar cheese, and 1 egg. Evenly spread mixture into prepared pie plate. In a medium bowl, combine remaining 3 eggs, broccoli, mushrooms, onion, and lemon pepper. Spread mixture in crust. Bake for 15 to 20 minutes. Sprinkle remaining ¼ cup Cheddar cheese evenly over top. Bake for additional 10 minutes. Place pie plate on a wire rack and let set for 10 minutes. Cut into 6 wedges.

HINT: 1⅓ cups uncooked rice usually cooks to about 2 cups.

Each serving equals:

HE: 1⅓ Protein (⅔ limited) • ⅔ Bread • ⅓ Vegetable

233 Calories • 9 gm Fat • 15 gm Protein •
23 gm Carbohydrate • 619 mg Sodium •
206 mg Calcium • 2 gm Fiber

DIABETIC: 2 Meat • 1 Starch • 1 Vegetable

Tomato Pot Pie

This inventive combination takes a classic family favorite—the pot pie—but stirs in entirely new ingredients for a taste sensation that's sure to please! In addition to that irresistible cheese-and-tomato flavor, you also get a healthy amount of protein and fiber.

Serves 6

> 1 cup finely chopped celery
> ½ cup finely chopped onion
> 1 (10¾-ounce) can Healthy Request Tomato Soup
> 3 cups (one 28-ounce can) tomatoes, coarsely chopped, drained, and ⅓ cup juice reserved
> 1 teaspoon dried parsley flakes
> 1½ cups (6 ounces) shredded Kraft reduced-fat Cheddar cheese ☆
> 1 (7.5-ounce) package Pillsbury refrigerated buttermilk biscuits

Preheat oven to 375 degrees. Spray an 8-by-8-inch baking dish with butter-flavored cooking spray. In a large skillet sprayed with butter-flavored cooking spray, sauté celery and onion for 10 minutes or just until vegetables are tender. Stir in tomato soup, reserved tomato juice, parsley flakes, and 1 cup Cheddar cheese. Continue cooking for 5 minutes or until cheese melts, stirring often. Add tomatoes. Mix well to combine. Spread mixture into prepared baking dish. Separate biscuits and cut each into 4 pieces. Evenly sprinkle biscuit pieces over tomato mixture. Lightly spray tops with butter-flavored cooking spray. Sprinkle remaining ½ cup Cheddar cheese over top. Bake 12 to 15 minutes or until biscuits are golden brown. Place baking dish on a wire rack and let set for 5 minutes. Divide into 6 servings.

HINT: If you like tomatoes on the sweeter side, stir in 1 tablespoon Sugar Twin when adding parsley flakes.

Each serving equals:

HE: 1½ Vegetable • 1⅓ Protein • 1¼ Bread •
¼ Slider • 10 Optional Calories

226 Calories • 6 gm Fat • 12 gm Protein •
31 gm Carbohydrate • 908 mg Sodium •
235 mg Calcium • 3 gm Fiber

DIABETIC: 1½ Starch • 1 Vegetable • 1 Meat

Cheesy Main Dish Strata

Three—count 'em—three cheeses in this gorgeous baked entree make it a mouthwatering choice, one your family is sure to request again and again. Even though it takes a bit more time to prepare than most of my recipes (not more work, just an extra hour or so in the fridge before baking!), it's definitely worth the wait!

☉ Serves 8

> 12 slices reduced-calorie Italian bread, cut into 1-inch cubes
> 1 (10¾-ounce) can Healthy Request Cream of Mushroom Soup
> ⅔ cup Carnation Nonfat Dry Milk Powder
> 1½ cups water
> 4 eggs, beaten, or equivalent in egg substitute
> ¼ cup (¾ ounce) grated Kraft fat-free Parmesan cheese
> 1½ cups (6 ounces) shredded Kraft reduced-fat Cheddar cheese
> 7 (¾-ounce) slices Kraft reduced-fat Swiss cheese, shredded

Spray a 9-by-13-inch baking dish with butter-flavored cooking spray. Evenly arrange bread cubes in prepared baking dish. In a large bowl, combine mushroom soup, dry milk powder, water, and eggs. Stir in Parmesan cheese, Cheddar cheese, and Swiss cheese. Pour soup mixture evenly over bread. Cover and refrigerate at least 1 hour or up to 24 hours. Uncover and bake at 350 degrees for 40 to 45 minutes or until a knife inserted near the center comes out clean. Place baking dish on a wire rack and let set for 5 minutes. Cut into 8 servings.

Each serving equals:

HE: 2½ Protein • ¾ Bread • ¼ Skim Milk • ¼ Slider • 1 Optional Calorie

---

244 Calories • 8 gm Fat • 20 gm Protein • 23 gm Carbohydrate • 668 mg Sodium • 451 mg Calcium • 4 gm Fiber

---

DIABETIC: 2 Meat • 1½ Starch/Carbohydrate

Cabbage and Potato Patties

Here's a simple dinner that belongs in your "Smart Leftovers" recipe section! I created this one evening when I spotted a bowl of leftover mashed potatoes and a bag of shredded cabbage in the refrigerator. You know how they say that necessity is the mother of invention? Well, this mother invented a lip-smacking meal to feed her family that was not only cost-effective but QUICK, QUICK, QUICK!

☻ Serves 4

½ cup finely chopped onion
2 cups cooked shredded cabbage
2 cups cold mashed potatoes
2 teaspoons reduced-calorie margarine

In a large bowl, combine onion, cabbage, and potatoes. Mix well to combine. Pat mixture into 4 patties. In a large skillet, melt margarine. Evenly arrange patties in skillet. Brown patties for 5 minutes on each side. Serve at once.

Each serving equals:

HE: 1¼ Vegetable • 1 Bread • ¼ Fat

109 Calories • 1 gm Fat • 3 gm Protein •
22 gm Carbohydrate • 334 mg Sodium •
48 mg Calcium • 3 gm Fiber

DIABETIC: 1 Vegetable • 1 Starch • ½ Fat

Garden Macaroni and Cheese Skillet

Here's a tasty and quick way to serve this beloved American classic with the addition of some healthy veggies! Stirred up on the stove top, it's just perfect to feed the healthy appetites of your busy family.

○ Serves 4 (1 cup)

> 1 (10¾-ounce) can Healthy Request Cream of Mushroom Soup
> ⅓ cup Carnation Nonfat Dry Milk Powder
> ½ cup water
> ¼ cup (¾ ounce) grated Kraft fat-free Parmesan cheese
> ¾ cup (3 ounces) shredded Kraft reduced-fat Cheddar cheese
> ¾ cup (3 ounces) shredded Kraft reduced-fat mozzarella cheese
> 2 cups hot cooked elbow macaroni, rinsed and drained
> 1 teaspoon dried parsley flakes
> ⅛ teaspoon black pepper
> 1 cup (one 8-ounce can) cut green beans, rinsed and drained
> 1 cup (one 8-ounce can) sliced carrots, rinsed and drained

In a large skillet sprayed with butter-flavored cooking spray, combine mushroom soup, dry milk powder, water, and Parmesan cheese. Stir in Cheddar and mozzarella cheeses. Cook over medium heat until cheeses melt, stirring often. Add macaroni, parsley flakes, and black pepper. Mix well to combine. Stir in green beans and carrots. Lower heat and simmer for 10 minutes, stirring occasionally.

HINT: 1⅓ cups uncooked elbow macaroni usually cooks to about 2 cups.

Each serving equals:

HE: 2¼ Protein • 1 Bread • 1 Vegetable •
¼ Skim Milk • ½ Slider • 1 Optional Calorie

313 Calories • 9 gm Fat • 20 gm Protein •
38 gm Carbohydrate • 813 mg Sodium •
452 mg Calcium • 3 gm Fiber

DIABETIC: 2 Meat • 2 Starch/Carbohydrate •
1 Vegetable

Southwest Corn Bake

If your kids relish a succulent corn pudding as much as mine do, then this should be a big hit at your house! It puffs up so beautifully and smells so good, they will gobble it down with grins on their faces— then maybe even offer to wash the car! ☻ Serves 4

⅔ cup Carnation Nonfat Dry Milk Powder
1 cup water
3 tablespoons all-purpose flour
1½ cups frozen whole-kernel corn, thawed
¾ cup (3 ounces) shredded Kraft reduced-fat Cheddar cheese
¼ cup chopped onion
¼ cup chunky salsa (mild, medium, or hot)
2 tablespoons chopped fresh parsley or 1 teaspoon dried parsley flakes
⅛ teaspoon black pepper
4 eggs or equivalent in egg substitute

Preheat oven to 350 degrees. Spray an 8-by-8-inch baking dish with butter-flavored cooking spray. In a covered jar, combine dry milk powder, water, and flour. Shake well to blend. Pour milk mixture into a medium saucepan sprayed with butter-flavored cooking spray. Cook over medium heat until mixture starts to thicken, stirring constantly. Stir in corn, cheese, onion, salsa, parsley, and black pepper. Continue cooking 2 to 3 minutes or until cheese melts. Remove from heat. Separate eggs. Stir yolks into corn mixture. In a large bowl, beat egg whites with an electric mixer until almost stiff. Fold ⅓ of beaten egg whites into corn mixture. Gently fold corn mixture into remaining egg whites. Pour mixture into prepared baking dish. Bake 40 to 45 minutes. Place baking dish on a wire rack and let set for 5 minutes. Divide into 4 servings.

Each serving equals:

HE: 1½ Protein (½ limited) • 1 Bread •
½ Skim Milk • ¼ Vegetable

214 Calories • 6 gm Fat • 15 gm Protein •
25 gm Carbohydrate • 330 mg Sodium •
314 mg Calcium • 2 gm Fiber

DIABETIC: 2 Meat • 1 Starch • ½ Skim Milk

Vegetable Enchiladas

Through the magic of microwavery, this dish arrives at your table in minutes—and utterly mouthwatering! There's just no substitute for serving tasty, fresh vegetables in today's favorite wrap, the tortilla, especially when they're topped with cheese and sour cream. Diet food? It sure doesn't look or taste like it!　　❍　　Serves 4

> 1 cup chopped fresh tomato
> 1/4 cup chopped onion
> 1/4 cup chopped green bell pepper
> 1 1/2 cups frozen or fresh whole-kernel corn
> 2 teaspoons reduced-calorie margarine
> 4 (6-inch) flour or corn tortillas
> 1/3 cup (1 1/2 ounces) shredded Kraft reduced-fat Cheddar cheese
> 1/4 cup Land O Lakes no-fat sour cream

In a 4-cup glass measuring cup, combine tomato, onion, green pepper, corn, and margarine. Microwave on MEDIUM (50% power) for 4 to 5 minutes. Spoon about 1/2 cup of the vegetable mixture on each tortilla. Evenly sprinkle about 1 1/2 tablespoons Cheddar cheese over each. Place tortillas in a microwavable baking dish and continue to microwave on MEDIUM for 2 to 3 minutes or until cheese melts. Top each with 1 tablespoon sour cream. Roll up and serve at once.

Each serving equals:

HE: 1 3/4 Bread • 3/4 Vegetable • 1/2 Protein • 1/4 Fat •
15 Optional Calories

---

209 Calories • 5 gm Fat • 8 gm Protein •
33 gm Carbohydrate • 285 mg Sodium •
99 mg Calcium • 2 gm Fiber

DIABETIC: 2 Starch • 1/2 Vegetable • 1/2 Meat

Mexican Pizza

Here's a fast and inexpensive kid-pleasing lunch that's easy, healthy, and oh-so-good. Pizza is so beloved by all the kids we feed at the local day care centers in DeWitt, Iowa, I created this dish with their hungry tummies in mind! ☻ Serves 4

4 (6-inch) flour tortillas
¼ cup Heinz Light Harvest Ketchup or any reduced-sodium
    ketchup
1 cup chunky salsa (mild, medium, or hot)
¾ cup (3 ounces) shredded Kraft reduced-fat Cheddar cheese

Preheat oven to 375 degrees. Spray a baking sheet with olive oil–flavored cooking spray. Place tortillas on prepared sheet. For each pizza, spread 1 tablespoon ketchup over a tortilla, spoon ¼ cup salsa over ketchup and top with 3 tablespoons Cheddar cheese. Bake for 15 minutes.

HINT: Good topped with 1 tablespoon Land O Lakes no-fat sour cream, but don't forget to count the few additional calories.

Each serving equals:

HE: 1 Bread • 1 Protein • ½ Vegetable •
15 Optional Calories

169 Calories • 5 gm Fat • 9 gm Protein •
22 mg Carbohydrate • 573 mg Sodium •
246 mg Calcium • 0 gm Fiber

DIABETIC: 1 Starch • 1 Meat • 1 Vegetable

Baked Omelet with Mushroom Sauce

Is breakfast or brunch time somewhat chaotic at your house? Nothing is ever ready at the same time, whether it's the eggs or the toast, and everyone tends to eat and run. Well, I hope this tasty dish will bring a little more peace and culinary pleasure to your table. I suggest preparing the first part of the recipe the night before, so when you wake up, you're ready to bake it and eat! 	☻	Serves 6

> 8 slices reduced-calorie bread, cut into 1-inch cubes
> ¾ cup (3 ounces) shredded Kraft reduced-fat Cheddar cheese
> 3 eggs or equivalent in egg substitute
> 3 cups skim milk ☆
> ¼ teaspoon lemon pepper
> 1 (10¾-ounce) can Healthy Request Cream of Mushroom Soup
> 1 teaspoon dried parsley flakes
> ¼ cup (¾ ounce) grated Kraft fat-free Parmesan cheese

Spray an 8-by-8-inch baking dish with butter-flavored cooking spray. Evenly arrange bread cubes in prepared baking dish. Sprinkle Cheddar cheese over top. In a large bowl, combine eggs, 2½ cups milk, and lemon pepper. Mix well using a wire whisk. Evenly pour egg mixture over bread and cheese. Cover and refrigerate for at least 1 hour or up to 24 hours. Uncover and bake at 350 degrees for 35 to 40 minutes, or until a knife inserted in center comes out clean. Just before omelet is done, in a small saucepan, combine mushroom soup, remaining ½ cup skim milk, parsley flakes, and Parmesan cheese. Cook over medium heat until mixture is heated through, stirring often. Cut omelet into 6 pieces. When serving, spoon about ¼ cup soup mixture over each piece.

Each serving equals:

HE: 1⅓ Protein (½ limited) • ⅔ Bread •
½ Skim Milk • ¼ Slider • 8 Optional Calories

222 Calories • 6 gm Fat • 16 gm Protein •
26 gm Carbohydrate • 653 mg Sodium •
322 mg Calcium • 4 gm Fiber

DIABETIC: 1 Meat • 1 Starch • ½ Skim Milk

Chili Pasta Grande

What's great about a recipe like this one is not only that it fits perfectly into your budget, but also that it's so full of crunch and flavor, no one will ever miss the meat! Pasta added to a traditional chili with beans provides additional texture and flavor, and also helps stretch the ingredients a little further. ☻ Serves 4 (1 cup)

½ cup chopped onion
½ cup chopped green bell pepper
1¾ cups (one 15-ounce can) Hunt's Chunky Tomato Sauce
2 teaspoons chili seasoning
1 tablespoon Brown Sugar Twin
1 teaspoon dried parsley flakes
½ cup Land O Lakes no-fat sour cream
10 ounces (one 16-ounce can) red kidney beans, rinsed and
    drained
2 cups hot cooked rotini pasta, rinsed and drained

In a large skillet sprayed with olive oil–flavored cooking spray, sauté onion and green pepper for 5 minutes or just until tender. Stir in tomato sauce, chili seasoning, Brown Sugar Twin, parsley flakes, and sour cream. Add kidney beans and rotini pasta. Mix well to combine. Lower heat and simmer for 5 minutes or until mixture is heated through, stirring often.

HINT: 1½ cups uncooked rotini pasta usually cooks to about 2 cups.

Each serving equals:

HE: 2¼ Vegetable • 1¼ Protein • 1 Bread •
¼ Skim Milk • 11 Optional Calories

212 Calories • 0 gm Fat • 9 gm Protein •
44 gm Carbohydrate • 743 mg Sodium •
61 mg Calcium • 8 gm Fiber

DIABETIC: 2 Vegetable • 2 Starch

Seafood

Here are some terrific ways to take canned fish like tuna, salmon, and shrimp—and make your hard-earned pennies work overtime to please your family! No one will ever guess that Salmon Cups with Creamed Peas is a budget recipe, nor will they feel they're getting any less than your best with such palate-pleasers as Tuna Rice à la King Skillet. Enjoy the bounty of the sea without spending an "ocean" of cash.

Seafood

Tuna-Cabbage Buns

Instead of serving tuna fish sandwiches with coleslaw on the side, I decided to blend the crunchy cabbage right in! This could be the start of a whole new tradition—a perfect "meal-in-a-bun"!

⚫ Serves 4

> 1 cup finely shredded cabbage
> 1 (6-ounce) can white tuna, packed in water, drained and flaked
> ⅓ cup Kraft fat-free mayonnaise
> 1 teaspoon dried parsley flakes
> 2 teaspoons dried onion flakes
> 4 reduced-calorie hamburger buns

In a small bowl, combine cabbage, tuna, mayonnaise, parsley flakes, and onion flakes. Mix well. For each sandwich, spoon about ½ cup tuna mixture between a bun. Serve at once or refrigerate until ready to serve.

Each serving equals:

HE: 1 Bread • ¾ Protein • ½ Vegetable •
13 Optional Calories

137 Calories • 1 gm Fat • 13 gm Protein •
19 gm Carbohydrate • 479 mg Sodium •
18 mg Calcium • 1 gm Fiber

DIABETIC: 1½ Meat • 1 Starch/Carbohydrate

Macaroni and Cheese-Tuna Salad Stuffed Tomatoes

Here's another fun combo that invites two already tasty foods to "tango" with a tomato! I like taking a dinner favorite like stuffed tomatoes and giving it that extra sparkle you don't expect. This might also be fun if you substituted shredded reduced-fat Swiss cheese for the Cheddar!   ☻   Serves 4

> 4 medium-sized fresh tomatoes
> 1 (6-ounce) can white tuna, packed in water, drained and flaked
> 1½ cups cold cooked elbow macaroni, rinsed and drained
> 1 cup diced celery
> 2 teaspoons dried onion flakes
> 1 teaspoon dried parsley flakes
> ½ cup Kraft fat-free mayonnaise
> ¼ cup (one 2-ounce jar) chopped pimiento, drained
> ⅓ cup (1½ ounces) shredded Kraft reduced-fat Cheddar cheese

Cut tops off tomatoes. Cut tomatoes into quarters, being careful not to cut all the way through the bottom. Spread wedges slightly apart. In a medium bowl, combine tuna, macaroni, celery, onion flakes, and parsley flakes. Add mayonnaise and pimiento. Mix well to combine. Stir in Cheddar cheese. Evenly spoon about ⅔ cup tuna mixture into center of each tomato. Serve at once or refrigerate until ready to serve.

HINT: 1 cup uncooked elbow macaroni usually cooks to about 1½ cups.

Each serving equals:

HE: 1½ Vegetable • 1¼ Protein • ¾ Bread • ¼ Slider

203 Calories • 3 gm Fat • 17 gm Protein •
27 gm Carbohydrate • 532 mg Sodium •
97 mg Calcium • 3 gm Fiber

DIABETIC: 1½ Meat • 1 Vegetable • 1 Starch

Tuna Skillet Pot Pie

Cliff really loved this top-of-the-stove surprise that's just right for steamy summer evenings when you'd rather not turn on your oven. It's delightfully creamy and cheesy, the biscuits are beautifully golden brown, and the flavor—well, it's simply out of this world!

○ Serves 6

2 (6-ounce) cans white tuna, packed in water, drained and flaked
1 cup frozen peas, thawed
1 (10¾-ounce) can Healthy Request Cream of Mushroom Soup
⅔ cup Carnation Nonfat Dry Milk Powder
¾ cup water
¾ cup Bisquick Reduced Fat Baking Mix
1 teaspoon dried parsley flakes
⅓ cup (1½ ounces) shredded Kraft reduced-fat Cheddar cheese

In a large skillet sprayed with butter-flavored cooking spray, combine tuna, peas, and mushroom soup. Cook over medium heat, stirring occasionally. Meanwhile, in a small bowl, combine dry milk powder and water. Stir ½ cup of milk mixture into tuna mixture. Lower heat and simmer while preparing biscuits. In a medium bowl, combine baking mix, parsley flakes, Cheddar cheese, and remaining ⅓ cup milk mixture. Mix just to combine. Using a full tablespoon as a guide, drop biscuit mixture onto tuna mixture to form 6 biscuits. Cover and continue simmering for 15 minutes or until biscuits are golden brown. Divide into 6 servings.

HINT: Thaw peas by placing in a colander and rinsing under hot water for one minute.

Each serving equals:

HE: 1⅓ Protein • 1 Bread • ⅓ Skim Milk •
¼ Slider • 8 Optional Calories

155 Calories • 3 gm Fat • 16 gm Protein •
16 gm Carbohydrate • 496 mg Sodium •
147 mg Calcium • 1 gm Fiber

DIABETIC: 2 Meat • 1½ Starch/Carbohydrate

Creamy Tuna and Vegetable Skillet

This is another super skillet combination that is just as mouthwatering as it is good for your bones! (Yes, it's got lots of healthy calcium, as well as so much nourishment for the dollar, you'll be amazed!) If you've vowed to add more fish meals to your menu, here's one the whole family will surely love. ☺ Serves 6 (1 cup)

1 (6-ounce) can white tuna, packed in water, drained and flaked
1 (10¾-ounce) can Healthy Request Cream of Celery Soup
⅓ cup skim milk
¾ cup (3 ounces) shredded Kraft reduced-fat Cheddar cheese
¼ cup (¾ ounce) grated Kraft fat-free Parmesan cheese
1 teaspoon dried parsley flakes
1 teaspoon dried onion flakes
¼ teaspoon black pepper
2 cups (one 16-ounce can) sliced carrots, rinsed and drained
2 cups (one 16-ounce can) cut green beans, rinsed and drained
½ cup (one 2.5-ounce jar) sliced mushrooms, drained
2 cups hot cooked noodles, rinsed and drained

In a large skillet, combine tuna, celery soup, and skim milk. Stir in Cheddar cheese, Parmesan cheese, parsley flakes, onion flakes, and black pepper. Cook over medium heat until cheese melts, stirring often. Add carrots, green beans, mushrooms, and noodles. Mix well to combine. Lower heat and simmer for 10 minutes, or until mixture is heated through, stirring often.

Each serving equals:

HE: 1½ Vegetable • 1⅓ Protein • ⅔ Bread •
¼ Slider • 8 Optional Calories

217 Calories • 5 gm Fat • 16 gm Protein •
27 gm Carbohydrate • 533 mg Sodium •
187 mg Calcium • 3 gm Fiber

DIABETIC: 2 Meat • 1½ Vegetable • 1½ Starch

Tuna Rice à la King Skillet

Even if the only royalty you're serving dinner to is the king of your castle (your hubby) or the little princess you call your daughter, here's a luscious and satisfying meal to please their palates (not to mention your own!). This cooks up so thick and rich, everyone will be dazzled.

● Serves 4 (1 cup)

2 cups skim milk

3 tablespoons all-purpose flour

½ cup (4 ounces) Philadelphia fat-free cream cheese

½ cup (one 2.5-ounce jar) sliced mushrooms, undrained

1 cup frozen peas, thawed

1 (6-ounce) can white tuna, packed in water, drained and flaked

1 teaspoon dried parsley flakes

¼ cup (one 2-ounce jar) chopped pimiento, drained

¼ teaspoon black pepper

1 cup (3 ounces) uncooked Minute Rice

In a covered jar, combine skim milk and flour. Shake well to blend. Pour milk mixture into a large skillet sprayed with butter-flavored cooking spray. Stir in cream cheese. Cook over medium heat until mixture starts to thicken, stirring constantly. Add undrained mushrooms, peas, tuna, parsley flakes, pimiento, and black pepper. Mix well to combine. Continue cooking just until mixture starts to boil. Stir in uncooked rice. Remove from heat. Cover and let set for 5 minutes. Fluff with a fork before serving.

HINT: Thaw peas by placing in a colander and rinsing under hot water for one minute.

Each serving equals:

HE: 1½ Bread • 1¼ Protein • ½ Skim Milk • ¼ Vegetable

233 Calories • 1 gm Fat • 27 gm Protein • 29 gm Carbohydrate • 552 mg Sodium • 172 mg Calcium • 3 gm Fiber

DIABETIC: 2 Meat • 1½ Starch • ½ Skim Milk

Heartland Tuna Bake

You heard it first in *The Music Man*—we Iowans can be quite stubborn, especially when it comes to tasty food! We just won't settle for less than the best we can get, even if we're working hard to make ends meet. But when we've got some "Iowa pride" (corn) to stir into a baked tuna entree, we're sure we couldn't do any better!

○ Serves 6

> 1½ cups finely chopped celery
> ½ cup chopped onion
> 1½ cups hot cooked rice
> 1½ cups frozen whole-kernel corn, thawed
> ⅔ cup Carnation Nonfat Dry Milk Powder
> ½ cup water
> 2 (6-ounce) cans white tuna, packed in water, drained and flaked
> ¾ cup (3 ounces) shredded Kraft reduced-fat Cheddar cheese
> 1 teaspoon dried parsley flakes
> ¼ teaspoon lemon pepper

Preheat oven to 325 degrees. Spray an 8-by-8-inch baking dish with butter-flavored cooking spray. In a large skillet sprayed with butter-flavored cooking spray, sauté celery and onion for 5 minutes or just until tender. Stir in rice and corn. In a small bowl, combine dry milk powder and water. Stir milk mixture into celery mixture. Add tuna, Cheddar cheese, parsley flakes, and lemon pepper. Mix well to combine. Pour mixture into prepared baking dish. Cover and bake for 45 minutes. Uncover and continue to bake an additional 10 minutes. Place baking dish on a wire rack and let set for 5 minutes. Divide into 6 servings.

HINT: 1 cup uncooked rice usually cooks to about 1½ cups.

Each serving equals:

HE: 1⅔ Protein • 1 Bread • ⅔ Vegetable •
⅓ Skim Milk

---

215 Calories • 3 gm Fat • 23 gm Protein •
24 gm Carbohydrate • 382 mg Sodium •
210 mg Calcium • 2 gm Fiber

DIABETIC: 2½ Meat • 1½ Starch/Carbohydrate

New Orleans Fish and Rice

The Cajuns of New Orleans have a motto: *"Laissez le bon temps rouler!"* Translated, it means, "Let the good times roll!" It's equally true when it comes to the foods they love—they're always good and spicy! By adding a touch of Southern heat, you too can bring those good times home! ☺ Serves 4

> ½ cup chopped onion
> 1 cup chopped green bell pepper
> 1¾ cups (one 15-ounce can) Hunt's Chunky Tomato Sauce
> ½ teaspoon dried minced garlic
> 1 teaspoon Tabasco sauce
> 1 tablespoon Brown Sugar Twin
> 2 teaspoons dried parsley flakes
> 16 ounces white fish, cut into 16 pieces
> 2 cups hot cooked rice

In a large skillet sprayed with butter-flavored cooking spray, sauté onion and green pepper for 5 minutes or until tender. Stir in tomato sauce, garlic, Tabasco sauce, Brown Sugar Twin, and parsley flakes. Add fish pieces. Mix gently to combine. Lower heat, cover, and simmer for 20 to 25 minutes, or until fish is tender, stirring occasionally. For each serving, place ½ cup rice on a plate and spoon about 1 full cup sauce mixture over top.

HINT: 1⅓ cups uncooked rice usually cooks to about 2 cups.

Each serving equals:

HE: 2½ Vegetable • 1½ Protein • 1 Bread • 1 Optional Calorie

213 Calories • 1 gm Fat • 25 gm Protein • 26 gm Carbohydrate • 796 mg Sodium • 57 mg Calcium • 3 gm Fiber

DIABETIC: 3 Meat • 2 Vegetable • 1 Starch

Seaside Spaghetti and Fish

Pasta and fish just seem right together—like sea and sand or hot dogs with mustard! Here's a fresh way to serve this classic dish: with a seafood twist that boosts the protein sky-high and delivers a succulent meal at a surprisingly low cost. Better than that, it's scrumptious!

● Serves 4

> 3 tablespoons all-purpose flour
> 1 teaspoon Italian seasoning
> 16 ounces white fish, cut into 16 pieces
> 2 tablespoons skim milk
> 1¾ cups (one 15-ounce can) Hunt's Chunky Tomato Sauce
> ½ cup chunky salsa (mild, medium, or hot)
> 2 cups hot cooked spaghetti, rinsed and drained
> ¼ cup (¾ ounce) grated Kraft fat-free Parmesan cheese

In a saucer, combine flour and Italian seasoning. Dip fish pieces in skim milk, then into flour mixture. (Reserve any remaining flour mixture.) Place fish in a large skillet sprayed with olive oil–flavored cooking spray. Brown fish pieces on both sides. In a medium bowl, combine tomato sauce, salsa, and any remaining flour mixture. Pour sauce mixture over fish. Lower heat, cover, and simmer for 20 to 25 minutes, or until fish is tender, stirring occasionally. For each serving, place ½ cup spaghetti on a plate, spoon about 1 full cup sauce mixture over top, and garnish with 1 tablespoon Parmesan cheese.

HINT: 1½ cups broken spaghetti usually cooks to about 2 cups.

Each serving equals:

> HE: 2 Vegetable • 1¾ Protein • 1¼ Bread •
> 3 Optional Calories
> ───────────────────────────────
> 266 Calories • 2 gm Fat • 27 gm Protein •
> 35 gm Carbohydrate • 1,019 mg Sodium •
> 98 mg Calcium • 4 gm Fiber
> ───────────────────────────────
> DIABETIC: 3½ Meat • 3 Vegetable • 1 Starch
> *or* 3½ Meat • 2 Starch • 1 Vegetable

Salmon Cups with Creamed Peas ❋

Looking for a lovely main dish to serve at a summer lunch for friends but can't afford anything with a fancy price? Here's a particularly pretty and delectable entree that looks special but isn't hard on your budget or your overbooked schedule!　⚫　Serves 6

1 (14½-ounce drained weight) can pink salmon, packed in water, drained and flaked

14 small fat-free saltine crackers, made into fine crumbs

1 egg or equivalent in egg substitute

1½ cups (one 12-fluid-ounce can) Carnation Evaporated Skim Milk☆

1 teaspoon dried onion flakes

2 teaspoons dried parsley flakes

3 tablespoons all-purpose flour

1½ cups frozen peas, thawed

¼ teaspoon lemon pepper

Preheat oven to 350 degrees. Spray a 6-hole muffin pan with butter-flavored cooking spray. In a medium bowl, combine salmon, cracker crumbs, egg, ¼ cup evaporated skim milk, onion flakes, and parsley flakes. Mix well. Evenly pat about ⅓ cup of salmon mixture into each prepared muffin cup. Press mixture up sides to form a cup. In a covered jar, combine remaining 1¼ cups evaporated skim milk and flour. Shake well to blend. Pour milk mixture into a medium saucepan sprayed with butter-flavored cooking spray. Add peas and lemon pepper. Mix well to combine. Cook over medium heat until mixture thickens, stirring often. Spoon about ⅓ cup of pea sauce into center of each salmon cup. Bake for 30 minutes. Place muffin pan on a wire rack and let set for 5 minutes.

HINTS:　1. A self-seal sandwich bag works great for crushing crackers.

　　　　2. Thaw peas by placing in a colander and rinsing under hot water for one minute.

Each serving equals:

HE: 2½ Protein • 1 Bread • ½ Skim Milk •
5 Optional Calories

---

195 Calories • 3 gm Fat • 21 gm Protein •
21 gm Carbohydrate • 508 mg Sodium •
295 mg Calcium • 2 gm Fiber

DIABETIC: 2½ Meat • 1 Starch • ½ Skim Milk

Shrimp and Vegetables

Ordering shrimp cocktail in restaurants means paying a high price for this beloved seafood treat. Why not enjoy the shrimp you love, but prepared at home in a tangy sauce and coupled with lots of delicious vegetables? You get the flavor you crave, but the only "belt-tightening" required will be when your healthy lifestyle means taking in the waist of your slacks! ☺ Serves 4 (1½ cups)

1 cup coarsely chopped onion
1 cup coarsely chopped green bell pepper
3 full cups (16 ounces) diced cooked potatoes
2 cups peeled and coarsely chopped fresh tomatoes
¼ cup shrimp sauce
½ teaspoon dried minced garlic
1 teaspoon dried parsley flakes
¼ teaspoon black pepper
2 (4.5-ounce drained weight) cans small shrimp, rinsed and drained

In a large skillet sprayed with olive oil–flavored cooking spray, sauté onion and green pepper for 5 minutes. Add potatoes. Mix well to combine. Simmer for 5 minutes, stirring often. Stir in tomatoes, shrimp sauce, garlic, parsley flakes, black pepper, and shrimp. Continue simmering for 5 minutes, stirring often.

HINT: 9 ounces frozen shrimp may be substituted for canned.

Each serving equals:

HE: 2¼ Protein • 2¼ Vegetable • 1 Bread • ¼ Slider • 5 Optional Calories

234 Calories • 2 gm Fat • 19 gm Protein • 35 gm Carbohydrate • 350 mg Sodium • 61 mg Calcium • 4 gm Fiber

DIABETIC: 1½ Vegetable • 1½ Starch • 1 Meat

Poultry

Remember that promise from the Depression years: "A chicken in every pot!"? That dream was something good in a tough time, a vision of hope that still rings true today, especially when you can economize and still relish such lively dishes as Cheesy Chicken and Green Beans over Noodles and Skillet Chicken Cacciatore. Make that old promise come delectably true when you serve up these dinnertime treats!

Poultry

Author's Note: Many of these recipes call for diced chicken or turkey, but if you don't have leftovers, purchase a chunk of cooked chicken breast or turkey breast from your local deli.

Hot Chicken Salad Sandwiches

Here's a fun new way to stir up a little lunchtime excitement at your house! By taking an American classic like chicken salad and adding a few extra touches (like the cheese), then baking the stuffed buns in the oven—you've got a great recipe for yum-yum-yum!

● Serves 6

1½ cups (8 ounces) diced cooked chicken breast
¾ cup (3 ounces) shredded Kraft reduced-fat Cheddar cheese
½ cup finely diced celery
¼ cup diced onion
2 tablespoons sweet pickle relish
½ cup Kraft fat-free mayonnaise
¼ cup (one 2-ounce jar) chopped pimiento
⅛ teaspoon black pepper
6 reduced-calorie hamburger buns

Preheat oven to 350 degrees. In a medium bowl, combine chicken, Cheddar cheese, celery, onion, and pickle relish. Add mayonnaise, pimiento, and black pepper. Mix gently to combine. Evenly spoon about ½ cup chicken mixture between each bun. Wrap each in foil. Arrange foil packages on a baking sheet and bake for 20 minutes.

Each serving equals:

HE: 2 Protein • 1 Bread • ¼ Vegetable •
13 Optional Calories

189 Calories • 5 gm Fat • 17 gm Protein •
19 gm Carbohydrate • 471 mg Sodium •
106 mg Calcium • 1 gm Fiber

DIABETIC: 2 Meat • 1 Starch

Skillet Chicken Stew

This stove-top stew has such a wonderfully old-fashioned flavor, your kids may wonder if Grandma stopped by to make dinner! By stirring in lots of veggies along with spaghetti noodles, you get tremendous chicken-y goodness out of a modest amount of meat.

◑ Serves 4 (1 full cup)

> 2 cups (one 16-ounce can) Healthy Request Chicken Broth
> 1 full cup (3 ounces) uncooked broken spaghetti
> 1 cup shredded carrots
> 1 cup chopped celery
> 2 cups shredded cabbage
> ½ cup chopped onion
> 1 full cup (6 ounces) diced cooked chicken breast
> ½ cup (one 2.5-ounce jar) sliced mushrooms, drained
> ¼ cup (one 2-ounce jar) chopped pimiento, drained
> 2 tablespoons reduced-sodium soy sauce

In a medium saucepan, bring chicken broth to a boil. Stir in uncooked spaghetti. Add carrots, celery, cabbage, and onion. Mix well to combine. Bring mixture to a boil. Lower heat and simmer for 15 minutes, stirring often. Stir in chicken, mushrooms, pimiento, and soy sauce. Continue simmering for 10 minutes, stirring occasionally.

Each serving equals:

HE: 2½ Vegetable • 1½ Protein • 1 Bread

166 Calories • 2 gm Fat • 18 gm Protein •
19 gm Carbohydrate • 627 mg Sodium •
41 mg Calcium • 3 gm Fiber

DIABETIC: 1½ Vegetable • 1½ Meat • 1 Starch

Cheesy Chicken and
Green Beans over Noodles

Each month, new "healthy" products appear in our local grocery stores, but many of them promise more than they deliver. One that really works great is the fat-free chicken gravy I used in this recipe, and I give it this high praise: if you didn't know it was fat-free, you'd never believe it!   ☾   Serves 4

½ cup finely chopped onion
1 (12-ounce) jar Heinz Fat Free Chicken Gravy
¼ cup (one 2-ounce jar) chopped pimiento, undrained
¾ cup (3 ounces) shredded Kraft reduced-fat Cheddar cheese
¼ teaspoon black pepper
1 teaspoon dried parsley flakes
1 cup (5 ounces) diced cooked chicken breast
2 cups (one 16-ounce can) cut green beans, rinsed and drained
2 cups hot cooked noodles, rinsed and drained

In a large skillet sprayed with butter-flavored cooking spray, sauté onion for 5 minutes or until just tender. Stir in chicken gravy, undrained pimiento, Cheddar cheese, black pepper, and parsley flakes. Continue cooking until cheese melts, stirring often. Add chicken and green beans. Mix well to combine. Lower heat and simmer for 5 minutes or until mixture is heated through, stirring occasionally. For each serving, place ½ cup noodles on a plate and spoon about ¾ cup chicken mixture over top.

HINT: 1¾ cups uncooked noodles usually cooks to about 2 cups.

Each serving equals:

HE: 2¼ Protein • 1¼ Vegetable • 1 Bread •
¼ Slider • 1 Optional Calorie

262 Calories • 6 gm Fat • 23 gm Protein •
29 gm Carbohydrate • 708 mg Sodium •
176 mg Calcium • 2 gm Fiber

DIABETIC: 2 Meat • 1½ Starch • 1 Vegetable

Fiesta Chicken Skillet

All across America, when it was time for Sunday supper, you'd often find a heaping platter of chicken and noodles carried steaming to the table! It's still one of the coziest main dishes anyone can serve, and I love discovering lively new ways to prepare it. This spicy version is a special favorite of my husband, Cliff's, and my son Tommy's—it must be the salsa!　　☺　　Serves 4 (1 cup)

> 1 full cup (6 ounces) diced cooked chicken breast
> ½ cup chunky salsa (mild, medium, or hot)
> 1 (12-ounce) jar Heinz Fat Free Chicken Gravy
> 2 cups hot cooked noodles, rinsed and drained
> 1 teaspoon dried parsley flakes

In a large skillet sprayed with olive oil–flavored cooking spray, combine chicken, salsa, and chicken gravy. Bring mixture to a boil. Add noodles and parsley flakes. Mix well to combine. Lower heat and simmer for 10 minutes or until mixture is heated through, stirring occasionally.

Each serving equals:

HE: 1½ Protein • 1 Bread • ¼ Vegetable • ¼ Slider • 18 Optional Calories

199 Calories • 3 gm Fat • 18 gm Protein • 25 gm Carbohydrate • 643 mg Sodium • 56 mg Calcium • 1 gm Fiber

DIABETIC: 1½ Meat • 1½ Starch • 1 Vegetable

Skillet Chicken Cacciatore

I think cooking with fat-free dressing is one of the thrifty chef's best secrets! It makes a wonderful marinade, and when stirred together with other tasty ingredients, it produces a family favorite like chicken cacciatore that's even better than the original! ☻ Serves 4

¼ cup Kraft Fat Free Italian Dressing
½ cup sliced onion
¼ cup sliced green bell pepper
16 ounces skinned and boned uncooked chicken breasts, cut into
    16 pieces
2 teaspoons Italian seasoning
2 teaspoons Sugar Twin or Sprinkle Sweet
1¾ cups (one 14 ½-ounce can) stewed tomatoes, undrained
2 cups hot cooked noodles, rinsed and drained

In a large skillet, heat Italian dressing. Add onion, green pepper, and chicken. Mix well to combine. Cook for 6 to 8 minutes, stirring occasionally. In a small bowl, combine Italian seasoning, Sugar Twin, and undrained stewed tomatoes. Spoon tomato mixture evenly over chicken. Lower heat and simmer for 12 to 15 minutes, or until chicken is tender, stirring occasionally. For each serving, place ½ cup noodles on a plate and spoon about 1 cup chicken mixture over top.

HINT: 1¾ cups uncooked noodles usually cooks to about 2 cups.

Each serving equals:

HE: 3 Protein • 1¾ Vegetable • 1 Bread •
9 Optional Calories

258 Calories • 2 gm Fat • 31 gm Protein •
29 gm Carbohydrate • 550 mg Sodium •
82 mg Calcium • 2 gm Fiber

DIABETIC: 3 Meat • 1½ Vegetable • 1 Starch

Nacho Chicken Potato Dish

Cutting corners never has to mean cutting back on flavor, and this spicy fiesta combination is a sizzling example! By drawing protein from three different sources (beans, cheese, and chicken), I never sacrifice on nutrition—but by stirring together lots of wonderful flavors, I create fireworks on a plate! ☻ Serves 6

> ¼ cup chopped onion
> ¼ cup chopped green bell pepper
> 1 full cup (6 ounces) diced cooked chicken breast
> 1 cup (one 8-ounce can) Hunt's Tomato Sauce
> 1 teaspoon taco seasoning
> 3 cups (10 ounces) shredded loose packed frozen potatoes
> 10 ounces (one 16-ounce can) red kidney beans, rinsed and
>   drained
> 1 (10¾-ounce) can Healthy Request Tomato Soup
> ½ cup chunky salsa (mild, medium, or hot)
> 1 teaspoon dried parsley flakes
> ¾ cup (3 ounces) shredded Kraft reduced-fat Cheddar cheese

Preheat oven to 350 degrees. Spray an 8-by-8-inch baking dish with olive oil–flavored cooking spray. In a large skillet sprayed with olive oil–flavored cooking spray, sauté onion and green pepper for 5 minutes. Stir in chicken, tomato sauce, and taco seasoning. Continue simmering for 2 to 3 minutes or until mixture is heated through. Spread mixture in prepared baking dish. Evenly layer potatoes and kidney beans over chicken mixture. In a small bowl, combine tomato soup, salsa, and parsley flakes. Spoon soup mixture evenly over top. Bake for 30 minutes. Sprinkle Cheddar cheese evenly over top. Continue baking for 10 to 15 minutes or until cheese melts. Place baking dish on a wire rack and let set for 5 minutes. Cut into 6 servings.

HINT: Mr. Dell's frozen shredded potatoes are a good choice. Raw shredded potatoes may be used in place of frozen potatoes.

Each serving equals:

HE: 2½ Protein • 1 Vegetable • ⅓ Bread • ¼ Slider •
10 Optional Calories

213 Calories • 5 gm Fat • 17 gm Protein •
25 gm Carbohydrate • 646 mg Sodium •
152 mg Calcium • 5 gm Fiber

DIABETIC: 2 Meat • 1½ Starch • 1 Vegetable

Chicken and Macaroni Stew

My kids always loved the kind of stove-top stews that filled the house with lip-smacking aromas like this one does! The ingredients are simple, the cooking time is short, but the payoff in flavor and soul satisfaction is off the charts! ☻ Serves 4 (1¾ cup)

> 1½ cups (8 ounces) diced cooked chicken breast
> ¼ cup chopped onion
> 1 cup (two 2.5-ounce jars) sliced mushrooms, drained
> 2 cups shredded carrots
> 2 cups frozen cut green beans, thawed
> 1¾ cups (one 14½-ounce can) stewed tomatoes, undrained
> 1½ cups water
> 1⅓ cups (3 ounces) uncooked elbow macaroni
> ½ teaspoon black pepper
> 2 teaspoons Italian seasoning

In a large skillet sprayed with olive oil–flavored cooking spray, sauté chicken and onion for 5 minutes. Add mushrooms, carrots, green beans, undrained stewed tomatoes, and water. Mix well to combine. Bring mixture to a boil. Stir in uncooked macaroni, black pepper, and Italian seasoning. Lower heat, cover, and simmer for 20 minutes or until macaroni is tender, stirring occasionally.

HINT: Thaw green beans by placing in a colander and rinsing under hot water for one minute.

Each serving equals:

HE: 3½ Vegetable • 2 Protein • 1 Bread

279 Calories • 3 gm Fat • 26 gm Protein •
37 gm Carbohydrate • 563 mg Sodium •
115 mg Calcium • 5 gm Fiber

DIABETIC: 3 Vegetable • 2 Meat • 1½ Starch

Chicken Cola Bake

You might think I let the kids take over the kitchen when I was creating this slightly strange but savory sauced chicken dish! I promise you, it sounds odd but the blend of diet cola, cream soup, and spices is simply marvelous! In fact, most people you serve it to will never believe there's cola in the gravy. . . .   ☻   Serves 4

> 16 ounces skinned and boned uncooked chicken breasts, cut into 4
>   pieces
> ½ cup Diet Pepsi or Diet Coke
> 1 (10¾-ounce) can Healthy Request Cream of Mushroom Soup
> 2 tablespoons dried onion flakes
> 1 tablespoon dried parsley flakes

Preheat oven to 350 degrees. Place chicken pieces in an 8-by-8-inch baking dish. In a medium bowl, combine diet cola, mushroom soup, onion flakes, and parsley flakes using a wire whisk. Pour soup mixture over chicken pieces. Cover and bake for 1 to 1½ hours, or until chicken is tender.

HINT: This "gravy" (the soup mixture without the chicken) is also delicious over rice or mashed potatoes.

Each serving equals:

HE: 3 Protein • ½ Slider • 10 Optional Calories

163 Calories • 3 gm Fat • 27 gm Protein •
7 gm Carbohydrate • 534 mg Sodium •
67 mg Calcium • 0 gm Fiber

DIABETIC: 3 Meat • ½ Starch/Carbohydrate

Baked Chicken in Sweet and Sour Sauce

Some like it sweet, and some like it tangy, but everyone who taste-tested this recipe gave it a perfect "10"! If you've always relished "sweet and sour" dishes but never tried one at home, give this scrumptious blend a whirl. ☻ Serves 4

> 16 ounces skinned and boned uncooked chicken breasts, cut into 4 pieces
> 1 tablespoon dried onion flakes
> ⅓ cup Kraft Fat Free French Dressing
> ¼ cup grape spreadable fruit
> 1 teaspoon dried parsley flakes

Preheat oven to 325 degrees. Spray an 8-by-8-inch baking dish with butter-flavored cooking spray. Evenly arrange chicken pieces in prepared baking dish. In a small bowl, combine onion flakes, French dressing, spreadable fruit, and parsley flakes. Evenly spoon mixture over chicken. Cover and bake for 30 minutes. Uncover and continue baking for 20 minutes or until chicken is tender. When serving, evenly spoon sauce over chicken pieces.

Each serving equals:

HE: 3 Protein • 1 Fruit • ¼ Slider • 13 Optional Calories

185 Calories • 1 gm Fat • 26 gm Protein • 18 gm Carbohydrate • 234 mg Sodium • 19 mg Calcium • 0 gm Fiber

DIABETIC: 3 Meat • 1 Fruit

Southern Delight Chicken Breasts ❄

Oh, no, JoAnna's cooking with soda again! Yes, I figured if chicken and cola went together like old friends, why not glaze a Southern-style chicken dish with this delightful combination? I bet your family will agree it's "finger-lickin'" good!   ◐   Serves 4

> 2 teaspoons reduced-calorie margarine
> 16 ounces skinless and boned uncooked chicken breasts, cut into 4 pieces
> ½ cup Diet 7UP☆
> ¼ cup apricot spreadable fruit
> 2 tablespoons (½ ounce) chopped pecans

In a large skillet, melt margarine. Arrange chicken pieces in skillet and brown for 4 to 5 minutes on each side. Reserve 1 tablespoon Diet 7UP. Pour remaining Diet 7UP over chicken. Lower heat, cover, and simmer for 15 minutes or until chicken is tender. In a small bowl, combine remaining 1 tablespoon Diet 7UP, spreadable fruit, and pecans. Evenly drizzle mixture over chicken pieces. Continue to simmer for 1 to 2 minutes or until sauce is heated through. When serving, drizzle sauce evenly over chicken pieces.

Each serving equals:

HE: 3 Protein • 1 Fruit • ¾ Fat

184 Calories • 4 gm Fat • 26 gm Protein •
11 gm Carbohydrate • 83 mg Sodium •
14 mg Calcium • 0 gm Fiber

DIABETIC: 3 Meat • 1 Fruit • 1 Fat

After the Holiday Turkey Casserole

If you're like me, you can never get enough turkey and stuffing! (And my kids agree!) Here's a smart and frugal way to use up those leftovers, but this flavorful casserole doesn't taste like the "day after"! It's amazingly creamy and rich, but still under 200 calories a serving!

☻ Serves 6

> 2 cups (one 16-ounce can) Healthy Request Chicken Broth ☆
> 1 cup chopped celery
> ½ cup chopped onion
> 1 cup frozen peas, thawed
> 1½ cups (3 ounces) unseasoned dry bread cubes
> 1½ cups (8 ounces) diced cooked turkey breast
> 1 teaspoon dried parsley flakes
> 1 teaspoon sage seasoning
> ⅛ teaspoon black pepper
> 1 (10¾-ounce) can Healthy Request Cream of Chicken Soup

Preheat oven to 350 degrees. Spray an 8-by-8-inch baking dish with butter-flavored cooking spray. In a large saucepan, combine 1 cup chicken broth, celery, and onion. Cook over medium heat until vegetables are just tender. Add peas, bread cubes, turkey, parsley flakes, sage seasoning, and black pepper. Mix well to combine. In a small bowl, combine remaining 1 cup chicken broth and chicken soup. Stir soup mixture into dressing mixture. Spoon mixture into prepared baking dish. Bake for 45 to 50 minutes. Place baking dish on a wire rack and let set for 5 minutes. Divide into 6 servings.

HINTS: 1. Thaw peas by placing in a colander and rinsing under hot water for one minute.

2. Pepperidge Farm bread cubes work great.

Each serving equals:

HE: 1⅓ Protein • 1 Bread • ½ Vegetable •
6 Optional Calories

179 Calories • 3 gm Fat • 17 gm Protein •
21 gm Carbohydrate • 553 mg Sodium •
22 mg Calcium • 2 gm Fiber

DIABETIC: 2 Meat • 1½ Starch/Carbohydrate

Mexican Turkey Noodle Bake

Turkey is such a healthy choice, you don't have to reserve it just for the holidays. I watch for sales on a whole turkey breast, then use it to stir up lots of dishes like this one. If you like it extra-spicy, add a pinch of extra chili seasoning, but don't set the kitchen on fire!

● Serves 8

> 1⅓ cups Carnation Nonfat Dry Milk Powder
> ½ cup water
> 1 (10¾-ounce) can Healthy Request Cream of Chicken Soup
> 1½ cups (8 ounces) diced cooked turkey breast
> 1¾ cups (one 14½-ounce can) stewed tomatoes, coarsely chopped
>   and undrained
> ¼ cup finely chopped onion
> 1 teaspoon dried parsley flakes
> 1 teaspoon chili seasoning
> 1 cup frozen whole-kernel corn, thawed
> 3 cups cooked noodles, rinsed and drained
> ¾ cup (3 ounces) shredded Kraft reduced-fat Cheddar cheese

Preheat oven to 350 degrees. Spray a 9-by-13-inch baking dish with olive oil–flavored cooking spray. In a large bowl, combine dry milk powder, water, and chicken soup. Add turkey, undrained stewed tomatoes, onion, parsley flakes, chili seasoning, and corn. Mix well to combine. Stir in noodles and Cheddar cheese. Pour mixture into prepared baking dish. Bake for 30 minutes. Place baking dish on a wire rack and let set for 5 minutes. Cut into 8 servings.

HINTS: 1. Thaw corn by placing in a colander and rinsing under hot water for one minute.

2. 2½ cups uncooked noodles usually cooks to about 3 cups.

Each serving equals:

HE: 1½ Protein • 1 Bread • ½ Skim Milk •
½ Vegetable • ¼ Slider • 3 Optional Calories

231 Calories • 3 gm Fat • 19 gm Protein •
32 gm Carbohydrate • 461 mg Sodium •
230 mg Calcium • 2 gm Fiber

DIABETIC: 2 Starch/Carbohydrate • 1½ Meat •
½ Vegetable

Baked Turkey and Rice

This cozy classic reminded me of eating at Grandma's in the days after Christmas, when she'd keep coming up with tasty new ways to finish up the holiday turkey! If this doesn't take you back to childhood memories with just one bite, I'll be very surprised!

● Serves 6

> 3 cups hot cooked rice
> 1½ cups (8 ounces) diced cooked turkey breast
> 1 (10¾-ounce) can Healthy Request Cream of Chicken Soup
> ½ cup (one 2.5-ounce jar) sliced mushrooms, drained
> ½ cup chopped onion
> ½ cup finely diced celery
> 1 tablespoon dried parsley flakes
> ¼ cup (one 2-ounce jar) chopped pimiento, drained
> ¼ cup Kraft fat-free mayonnaise
> ⅛ teaspoon black pepper

Preheat oven to 350 degrees. Spray an 8-by-8-inch baking dish with butter-flavored cooking spray. In a large bowl, combine rice, turkey, and chicken soup. Stir in mushrooms, onion, celery, parsley flakes, pimiento, mayonnaise, and black pepper. Mix well to combine. Pour mixture into prepared baking dish. Bake for 60 minutes. Place baking dish on a wire rack and let set for 5 minutes. Divide into 6 servings.

HINT: 2 cups uncooked rice usually cooks to about 3 cups.

Each serving equals:

HE: 1⅓ Protein • 1 Bread • ⅔ Vegetable • ¼ Slider • 13 Optional Calories

186 Calories • 2 gm Fat • 15 gm Protein • 27 gm Carbohydrate • 296 mg Sodium • 24 mg Calcium • 1 gm Fiber

DIABETIC: 1½ Starch/Carbohydrate • 1½ Meat

Home-Style Turkey with Biscuits

Here's an old-fashioned dish served with new-style smarts no thrifty cook can afford to be without! Healthy prepared foods like the soup and ready-made biscuits let you save money and save time—and who doesn't need to do both? ☺ Serves 6

1½ cups (8 ounces) diced cooked turkey breast
1 (10¾-ounce) can Healthy Request Cream of Chicken Soup
1 teaspoon dried onion flakes
1 teaspoon dried parsley flakes
1 cup (one 8-ounce can) sliced carrots, rinsed and drained
1 cup (one 8-ounce can) cut green beans, rinsed and drained
1 (7.5-ounce) can Pillsbury refrigerated buttermilk biscuits
¼ teaspoon paprika

Preheat oven to 400 degrees. Spray an 8-by-8-inch baking dish with butter-flavored cooking spray. In a large skillet, combine turkey, chicken soup, onion flakes, parsley flakes, carrots, and green beans. Cook over medium heat for 10 minutes, stirring often. Spread hot mixture into prepared baking dish. Separate biscuits and cut each into 4 pieces. Evenly sprinkle biscuit pieces over top of turkey mixture. Lightly spray tops of biscuit pieces with butter-flavored cooking spray. Sprinkle paprika evenly over top. Bake for 15 minutes or until biscuits are golden brown. Place baking dish on a wire rack and let set for 2 to 3 minutes. Divide into 6 servings.

Each serving equals:

HE: 1⅓ Protein • 1¼ Bread • ⅔ Vegetable • ¼ Slider • 10 Optional Calories

191 Calories • 3 gm Fat • 17 gm Protein • 24 gm Carbohydrate • 546 mg Sodium • 20 mg Calcium • 2 gm Fiber

DIABETIC: 1½ Meat • 1½ Starch • 1 Vegetable

Cozy Turkey Pot Pies

This is a wonderful recipe to serve on cold winter afternoons when your kids come in from playing in the snow. It tastes delectably homemade and warms the coldest child through and through.

○ Serves 4

> 1½ cups (8 ounces) diced cooked turkey breast
> ½ cup (one 2.5-ounce jar) sliced mushrooms, drained
> ½ cup chopped onion
> 1 cup frozen peas, thawed
> ¼ teaspoon black pepper
> ⅓ cup (1½ ounces) shredded Kraft reduced-fat Cheddar cheese
> 6 tablespoons all-purpose flour
> 2 teaspoons baking powder
> 2 teaspoons dried parsley flakes
> 1 cup skim milk
> 2 eggs or equivalent in egg substitute
> 2 tablespoons Kraft fat-free mayonnaise

Preheat oven to 400 degrees. Spray 4 individual casseroles or (10-ounce) custard cups with butter-flavored cooking spray. In a medium bowl, combine turkey, mushrooms, onion, peas, black pepper, and Cheddar cheese. Evenly divide mixture among prepared casseroles. In a small bowl, combine flour, baking powder, and parsley flakes. Add skim milk, egg, and mayonnaise. Mix well to combine. Evenly spoon batter over top of casseroles. Bake for 30 to 35 minutes. Place casseroles on a wire rack and let set for 5 minutes.

HINT: Thaw peas by placing in a colander and rinsing under hot water for one minute.

Each serving equals:

HE: 3 Protein (½ limited) • 1 Bread • ½ Vegetable • ¼ Skim Milk • 5 Optional Calories

279 Calories • 7 gm Fat • 30 gm Protein • 24 gm Carbohydrate • 681 mg Sodium • 331 mg Calcium • 4 gm Fiber

DIABETIC: 3 Meat • 1½ Starch • ½ Vegetable

Beef

Here's a group of recipes that prove without a doubt how a little of something good can go a long, long way toward filling your family's tummies without emptying your purse! The healthiest extra-lean beef costs a bit more, but when just half a pound serves four so well, you'll be saving money when it counts. When they want to know "Where's the beef?" show them how thrifty can still mean tasty with such delights as Campfire Chili Burgers and Creamy Baked Tacos.

Beef

Campfire Chili Burgers

Here's a clever way to stretch your meat budget a little—and to "stuff" lots of tangy flavor into an American classic! If you've never considered serving chili on a bun, keep this recipe handy for your next family camping trip. ☻ Serves 6

16 ounces ground 90% lean turkey or beef
½ cup chopped onion
½ cup chunky salsa (mild, medium, or hot)
6 ounces (one 8-ounce can) kidney beans, rinsed and drained
¼ cup Heinz Light Harvest Ketchup or any reduced-sodium ketchup
1 teaspoon chili seasoning
6 reduced-calorie hamburger buns

In a large skillet sprayed with butter-flavored cooking spray, brown meat and onion. Add salsa, kidney beans, ketchup, and chili seasoning. Mix well to combine. Lower heat and simmer for 10 minutes, stirring occasionally. For each sandwich, spoon a full ⅓ cup mixture between a bun.

Each serving equals:

HE: 2½ Protein • 1 Bread • ⅓ Vegetable • 17 Optional Calories

---

223 Calories • 7 gm Fat • 17 gm Protein • 23 gm Carbohydrate • 307 mg Sodium • 40 mg Calcium • 3 gm Fiber

---

DIABETIC: 2 Meat • 1 Starch • ½ Vegetable

Grande Fiesta Burgers

Spicy, crunchy, tangy—and served up fast! This is a great budget meal that doesn't taste like you're watching the purse strings. The secret—abundant flavor makes a meal taste like a banquet!

○ Serves 6

16 ounces ground 90% lean turkey or beef
½ cup chopped onion
½ cup chopped green bell pepper
1 (10¾-ounce) can Healthy Request Tomato Soup
2 teaspoons chili seasoning
1 teaspoon dried parsley flakes
¼ teaspoon black pepper
6 reduced-calorie hamburger buns

In a large skillet sprayed with olive oil–flavored cooking spray, brown meat, onion, and green pepper. Add tomato soup, chili seasoning, parsley flakes, and black pepper. Mix well to combine. Lower heat and simmer for 10 minutes, stirring occasionally. For each serving, spoon a full ⅓ cup meat mixture between a bun.

Each serving equals:

HE: 2 Protein • 1 Bread • ⅓ Vegetable • ¼ Slider • 10 Optional Calories

224 Calories • 8 gm Fat • 16 gm Protein • 22 gm Carbohydrate • 385 mg Sodium • 11 mg Calcium • 2 gm Fiber

DIABETIC: 2 Meat • 1½ Starch

Skillet Pizza Burgers

Pizza burgers were always a favorite of my boys when they were growing up, so when I asked them to taste this healthy version of their childhood treat, I held my breath for a moment. Phew! They absolutely loved it—and I bet your kids will too!

○ Serves 6

16 ounces ground 90% lean turkey or beef

6 tablespoons (1½ ounces) dried fine bread crumbs

½ cup finely chopped onion

⅛ teaspoon black pepper

1½ teaspoons Italian seasoning

¼ cup Heinz Light Harvest Ketchup or any reduced-sodium ketchup

3 (¾-ounce) slices Kraft reduced-fat mozzarella cheese

6 lettuce leaves

1 medium-sized fresh tomato, cut into 6 slices

6 reduced-calorie hamburger buns

In a large bowl, combine meat, bread crumbs, onion, black pepper, Italian seasoning, and ketchup. Mix well to combine. Using a ⅓ cup measuring cup as a guide, form into 6 patties. Arrange patties in a large skillet sprayed with olive oil–flavored cooking spray. Brown for 4 to 5 minutes on each side or until cooked to desired doneness. Cut mozzarella cheese slices in half. Place 1 piece of cheese on each patty and continue cooking for 1 minute or until cheese melts. For each sandwich, place a lettuce leaf and a tomato slice on bun bottom, arrange meat patty over tomato, and place bun top over meat.

Each serving equals:

HE: 2½ Protein • 1⅓ Bread • ⅓ Vegetable • 10 Optional Calories

257 Calories • 9 gm Fat • 20 gm Protein • 24 gm Carbohydrate • 359 mg Sodium • 91 mg Calcium • 2 gm Fiber

DIABETIC: 2 Meat • 1½ Starch/Carbohydrate

Southwestern Meat Loaf

As Cliff and I have driven all across America to share my Healthy Exchanges recipes, we've thoroughly enjoyed tasting regional variations of traditional recipes. When I stirred cornmeal instead of bread crumbs into this meat loaf mix, it brought back tasty memories of our time in the Southwest. ☻ Serves 6

16 ounces ground 90% lean turkey or beef
¼ cup (1½ ounces) yellow cornmeal
½ cup finely chopped onion
½ cup finely chopped green bell pepper
1¾ cups (one 15-ounce can) Hunt's Chunky Tomato Sauce☆
1½ teaspoons chili seasoning
1 tablespoon Brown Sugar Twin
1 teaspoon dried parsley flakes
¼ teaspoon dried minced garlic

Preheat oven to 350 degrees. Spray an 8-by-8-inch baking dish with olive oil–flavored cooking spray. In a large bowl, combine meat, cornmeal, onion, green pepper, ¼ cup tomato sauce, and chili seasoning. Mix well to combine. Pat mixture into prepared baking dish. In a small bowl, combine remaining 1½ cups tomato sauce, Brown Sugar Twin, parsley flakes, and garlic. Pour mixture evenly over meat loaf. Bake for 50 to 55 minutes. Place baking dish on a wire rack and let set for 5 minutes. Cut into 6 servings.

Each serving equals:

HE: 2 Protein • 1½ Vegetable • ⅓ Bread •
1 Optional Calorie

154 Calories • 6 gm Fat • 15 gm Protein •
10 gm Carbohydrate • 539 mg Sodium •
5 mg Calcium • 2 gm Fiber

DIABETIC: 2 Meat • 1 Vegetable • ½ Starch

Budgetville Meat Loaf

Most of my life I've lived in "Budgetville," stretching limited dollars to feed my family. Even now, though it's just Cliff and me, I still tend to shop the sales and plan menus with an eye to economy. But with dishes like this appetizing meat loaf, frugal can still mean flavorful!

● Serves 6

⅔ cup Carnation Nonfat Dry Milk Powder

¾ cup water

2 teaspoons dried parsley flakes

1 teaspoon lemon juice

2 tablespoons dried onion flakes

1 teaspoon prepared mustard

⅛ teaspoon dried minced garlic

16 ounces ground 90% lean turkey or beef

½ cup + 1 tablespoon dried fine bread crumbs

Preheat oven to 350 degrees. Spray a 9-by-5-inch loaf pan with butter-flavored cooking spray. In a large bowl, combine dry milk powder, water, parsley flakes, lemon juice, onion flakes, mustard, and garlic. Add meat and bread crumbs. Mix well to combine. Pat mixture into prepared pan. Bake for 1 hour. Place pan on a wire rack and let set for 5 minutes. Cut into 6 servings.

Each serving equals:

HE: 2 Protein • ½ Bread • ⅓ Skim Milk

---

175 Calories • 7 gm Fat • 17 gm Protein • 11 gm Carbohydrate • 193 mg Sodium • 113 mg Calcium • 0 gm Fiber

---

DIABETIC: 2 Meat • ½ Starch/Carbohydrate
or 2 Meat • ½ Skim Milk

Mexican Tomato Meat Loaf Bake ❄

Yes, I'm actually telling you that nacho chips can be part of a healthy lifestyle—isn't it amazing! As long you keep moderation as your watchword, you can treat your taste buds to such formerly forbidden foods. This spicy recipe won applause from Cliff, who loves Mexican food enough to eat it every day. ☻   Serves 6

16 ounces ground 90% lean turkey or beef
1¾ cups (one 14½-ounce can) stewed tomatoes, coarsely chopped
    and undrained
2 tablespoons chili seasoning
½ cup (1½ ounces) crushed Doritos Reduced Fat Nacho Chips
¾ cup chopped green bell pepper
½ cup chopped onion
⅓ cup (1½ ounces) shredded Kraft reduced-fat Cheddar cheese

Preheat oven to 375 degrees. Spray an 8-by-8-inch baking dish with butter-flavored cooking spray. In a medium bowl, combine meat, undrained stewed tomatoes, chili seasoning, nacho chips, green pepper, and onion. Spread mixture into prepared baking dish. Bake for 40 to 45 minutes. Evenly sprinkle Cheddar cheese over top and continue baking for 5 minutes or until cheese melts. Place baking dish on a wire rack and let set for 5 minutes. Divide into 6 servings.

HINTS: Good served with 1 tablespoon Land O Lakes no-fat sour cream, but don't forget to count the few additional calories.

Each serving equals:

HE: 2⅓ Protein • 1 Vegetable • ⅓ Bread

207 Calories • 9 gm Fat • 17 gm Protein •
12 gm Carbohydrate • 394 mg Sodium •
92 mg Calcium • 1 gm Fiber

DIABETIC: 2 Meat • 1 Vegetable • ½ Starch

Grande Spaghetti Skillet

Here's another stove-top sensation that combines ordinary ingredients from your pantry shelves into a dish with so much flavor I called it "grande"! Sure, you could serve spaghetti a couple times a week as a cost-cutter, but why settle for the same old thing when you can "live a little"! ☺ Serves 6 (1 full cup)

> 8 ounces ground 90% lean turkey or beef
> ½ cup chopped onion
> ¼ cup chopped green bell pepper
> 2 cups hot cooked spaghetti, rinsed and drained
> 6 ounces (one 8-ounce can) kidney beans, rinsed and drained
> 1 cup frozen whole kernel corn, thawed
> 1¾ cups (one 14½-ounce can) stewed tomatoes, undrained
> 1 cup (one 8-ounce can) Hunt's Tomato Sauce
> ⅔ cup (2¼ ounces) shredded Kraft reduced-fat Cheddar cheese
> 2 teaspoons chili seasoning
> ⅛ teaspoon black pepper
> 6 tablespoons Land O Lakes no-fat sour cream

In a large skillet sprayed with olive oil–flavored cooking spray, brown meat, onion and green pepper. Add spaghetti, kidney beans, corn, undrained stewed tomatoes, and tomato sauce. Mix well to combine. Stir in Cheddar cheese, chili seasoning, and black pepper. Lower heat and simmer for 10 to 15 minutes, stirring occasionally. When serving, top each with 1 tablespoon sour cream.

HINT: 1½ cups broken uncooked spaghetti usually cooks to about 2 cups.

Each serving equals:

HE: 2⅓ Protein • 1½ Vegetable • 1 Bread •
15 Optional Calories

225 Calories • 5 gm Fat • 15 gm Protein •
30 gm Carbohydrate • 395 mg Sodium •
105 mg Calcium • 4 gm Fiber

DIABETIC: 2 Meat • 1½ Vegetable • 1½ Starch

Italian Hamburger Milk Gravy with Green Beans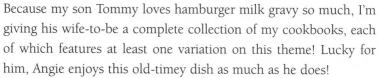

Because my son Tommy loves hamburger milk gravy so much, I'm giving his wife-to-be a complete collection of my cookbooks, each of which features at least one variation on this theme! Lucky for him, Angie enjoys this old-timey dish as much as he does!

◐ Serves 4 (1 cup)

> 8 ounces ground 90% lean turkey or beef
> 1½ cups (one 12-fluid-ounce can) Carnation Evaporated Skim Milk
> 3 tablespoons all-purpose flour
> 2 cups (one 16-ounce can) French-style green beans, rinsed and drained
> ½ cup (one 2.5-ounce jar) sliced mushrooms, drained
> 1 teaspoon Italian seasoning
> 1 teaspoon dried onion flakes
> ⅛ teaspoon black pepper

In a large skillet sprayed with butter-flavored cooking spray, brown meat. In a covered jar, combine evaporated skim milk and flour. Shake well to blend. Pour milk mixture into meat mixture. Mix well to combine. Stir in green beans, mushrooms, Italian seasoning, onion flakes, and black pepper. Lower heat and simmer for 10 minutes, or until mixture is heated through, stirring occasionally.

Each serving equals:

HE: 1½ Protein • 1¼ Vegetable • ¾ Skim Milk • ¼ Bread

---

209 Calories • 5 gm Fat • 20 gm Protein •
21 gm Carbohydrate • 249 mg Sodium •
311 mg Calcium • 2 gm Fiber

DIABETIC: 1½ Meat • 1 Vegetable • 1 Skim Milk

Supper-Time Rice Skillet

If you're looking for inexpensive dishes that supply the people you love with plenty of calcium, seek no further than this stove-top special! It's simple, it's tasty, and it will make your family feel wonderfully satisfied. Only you need to know how good it is for them!

● Serves 4 (1 cup)

> 8 ounces ground 90% lean turkey or beef
> ½ cup chopped onion
> 1½ cups finely chopped celery
> ½ cup (one 2.5-ounce jar) sliced mushrooms, drained
> 1⅓ cups (4 ounces) uncooked Minute Rice
> 1 (10¾-ounce) can Healthy Request Cream of Mushroom Soup
> ¼ cup (one 2-ounce jar) chopped pimiento, undrained
> 1⅓ cups skim milk

In a large skillet sprayed with butter-flavored cooking spray, brown meat, onion, and celery for 10 minutes or until celery is tender. Add mushrooms, uncooked rice, mushroom soup, undrained pimiento, and skim milk. Mix well to combine. Lower heat, cover, and simmer for 10 minutes, or until rice is tender, stirring occasionally.

Each serving equals:

HE: 1½ Protein • 1¼ Vegetable • 1 Bread •
¼ Skim Milk • ½ Slider • 1 Optional Calorie

223 Calories • 7 gm Fat • 15 gm Protein •
25 gm Carbohydrate • 513 mg Sodium •
174 mg Calcium • 2 gm Fiber

DIABETIC: 1½ Meat • 1½ Starch/Carbohydrate •
½ Vegetable

Baked Adobe Vegetable Stew

This casserole brings together lots of Southwestern flavor in a dish that's so savory, no one will notice they're getting just a touch of meat amidst all those healthy veggies and noodles! Maybe the Food Pyramid was built from this kind of "adobe"? ☻ Serves 6

> 8 ounces ground 90% lean turkey or beef
> ½ cup chopped onion
> 1 cup (one 8-ounce can) Hunt's Tomato Sauce
> ½ cup chunky salsa (mild, medium, or hot)
> 2 tablespoons Brown Sugar Twin
> 2 cups hot cooked noodles, rinsed and drained
> 2 cups (one 16-ounce can) cut green beans, rinsed and drained
> 2 cups (one 16-ounce can) sliced carrots, rinsed and drained
> ½ cup frozen peas, thawed
> ½ cup frozen corn, thawed
> ¾ cup (3 ounces) shredded Kraft reduced-fat Cheddar cheese

Preheat oven to 350 degrees. Spray an 8-by-8-inch baking dish with olive oil–flavored cooking spray. In a large skillet sprayed with olive oil–flavored cooking spray, brown meat and onion. Add tomato sauce, salsa, and Brown Sugar Twin. Mix well to combine. Lower heat and simmer for 10 minutes, stirring occasionally. Stir in noodles, green beans, carrots, peas, and corn. Pour mixture into prepared baking dish. Sprinkle Cheddar cheese evenly over top. Bake for 25 to 30 minutes. Place baking dish on a wire rack and let set for 5 minutes. Divide into 6 servings.

HINTS: 1. 1¾ cups uncooked noodles usually cooks to about 2 cups.

2. Thaw peas and corn by placing in a colander and rinsing under hot water for one minute.

Each serving equals:

HE: 2⅓ Vegetable • 1 Protein • 1 Bread •
1 Optional Calorie

---

222 Calories • 6 gm Fat • 15 gm Protein •
27 gm Carbohydrate • 532 mg Sodium •
165 mg Calcium • 4 gm Fiber

DIABETIC: 2 Vegetable • 1½ Meat • 1 Starch

Goulash Jumble

Part of my heritage is Eastern European, where hearty main dishes are always on the menu! Here's an easy combo your family is sure to relish, especially if they love the taste of cabbage cooked in a succulent broth until it's full of flavor! ☻ Serves 6 (1 cup)

16 ounces ground 90% lean turkey or beef
1¾ cups (one 15-ounce can) Hunt's Chunky Tomato Sauce
2 cups shredded cabbage
1 cup (one 8-ounce can) sliced carrots, rinsed and drained
1 cup hot cooked elbow macaroni, rinsed and drained
1¾ cups (one 14½-ounce can) Swanson Beef Broth
3 tablespoons all-purpose flour
⅔ cup Carnation Nonfat Dry Milk Powder
1 teaspoon dried onion flakes
1 teaspoon dried parsley flakes

In a large skillet sprayed with butter-flavored cooking spray, brown meat. Stir in tomato sauce, cabbage, carrots, and macaroni. In a covered jar, combine beef broth, flour, dry milk powder, onion flakes, and parsley flakes. Shake well to blend. Pour broth mixture into meat mixture. Mix well to combine. Lower heat and simmer for 15 minutes, stirring occasionally.

HINT: ⅔ cup uncooked elbow macaroni usually cooks to about 1 cup.

Each serving equals:

HE: 2 Protein • 2 Vegetable • ½ Bread •
⅓ Skim Milk • 6 Optional Calories

---

201 Calories • 7 gm Fat • 19 gm Protein •
20 gm Carbohydrate • 832 mg Sodium •
109 mg Calcium • 2 gm Fiber

DIABETIC: 2 Meat • 2 Vegetable • ½ Starch
or 2 Meat • ½ Starch/Carbohydrate

Easy Skillet Stew

Okay, it's not a special occasion, it's just the family around the table, so what's for dinner? Why not stir up this simple but satisfying meat-and-potatoes combination that answers the question perfectly? ☻ Serves 4 (full 1 cup)

> 8 ounces ground 90% lean turkey or beef
> ½ cup chopped onion
> 1½ cups chopped celery
> 2 cups frozen cut carrots, thawed
> 1¾ cups (one 14½-ounce can) Swanson Beef Broth
> 10 ounces (one 16-ounce can) sliced cooked potatoes, rinsed and
>   drained
> 1 (10¾-ounce) can Healthy Request Tomato Soup
> 1 teaspoon dried parsley flakes
> ¼ teaspoon black pepper

In a large skillet sprayed with butter-flavored cooking spray, brown meat. Stir in onion, celery, carrots, and beef broth. Cook over medium heat for about 20 minutes or until liquid is almost absorbed, stirring occasionally. Add potatoes, tomato soup, parsley flakes, and black pepper. Mix well to combine. Lower heat and simmer for 5 minutes or until mixture is heated through, stirring often.

Each serving equals:

HE: 2 Vegetable • 1½ Protein • ⅔ Bread • ½ Slider • 13 Optional Calories

229 Calories • 5 gm Fat • 14 gm Protein • 32 gm Carbohydrate • 612 mg Sodium • 43 mg Calcium • 4 gm Fiber

DIABETIC: 1½ Meat • 1½ Starch • 1 Vegetable

Heritage Corn Casserole

This is just the kind of wonderful and economical casserole my mother used to fix when she had to make one egg and a half pound of meat serve the whole family. Homemade bread crumbs give this classic baked corn dish a real old-time taste. ❂ Serves 4

> 8 ounces ground 90% lean turkey or beef
> 2 cups (one 16-ounce can) whole-kernel corn, rinsed and drained
> 1 egg, beaten, or equivalent in egg substitute
> ⅓ cup water
> ⅓ cup Carnation Nonfat Dry Milk Powder
> ½ cup chopped onion
> 1½ teaspoons taco seasoning
> ¼ teaspoon black pepper
> 1 teaspoon dried parsley flakes
> 2 slices reduced-calorie white bread, made into crumbs

Preheat oven to 350 degrees. Spray an 8-by-8-inch baking dish with butter-flavored cooking spray. In a large skillet sprayed with butter-flavored cooking spray, brown meat. Remove from heat. In a large bowl, combine corn, egg, water and dry milk powder. Stir in onion, taco seasoning, black pepper, and parsley flakes. Add browned meat and bread crumbs. Mix gently to combine. Spread mixture into prepared baking dish. Bake for 40 to 45 minutes. Place baking dish on a wire rack and let set for 5 minutes. Divide into 4 servings.

Each serving equals:

HE: 1¾ Protein (¼ limited) • 1¼ Bread • ¼ Skim Milk • ¼ Vegetable

226 Calories • 6 gm Fat • 17 gm Protein • 26 gm Carbohydrate • 163 mg Sodium • 92 mg Calcium • 4 gm Fiber

DIABETIC: 2 Meat • 1½ Starch

Pizza Lover's Pizza

If making your own pizza just seemed like too much trouble, I'm here to tell you that it isn't any longer! You'll never taste fresher ingredients piled on a fresh-baked golden crust than when you try this recipe for homemade happiness. Invite your kids to help by sprinkling the veggies and cheese on top! ☻   Serves 8

> 16 ounces ground 90% lean turkey or beef
> 1 (11-ounce) can Pillsbury Crusty French Loaf
> 1¾ cups (one 15-ounce can) Hunt's Chunky Tomato Sauce
> 1 teaspoon Italian seasoning
> ½ cup chopped onion
> ½ cup chopped green bell pepper
> ½ cup (2 ounces) sliced ripe olives
> ½ cup (one 2.5-ounce jar) sliced mushrooms, drained
> ¾ cup (3 ounces) shredded Kraft reduced-fat Cheddar cheese
> ¾ cup (3 ounces) shredded Kraft reduced-fat mozzarella cheese

Preheat oven to 425 degrees. In a large skillet sprayed with olive oil–flavored cooking spray, brown meat. Meanwhile, spray a 10-by-15-inch baking sheet with olive oil–flavored cooking spray. Unroll French loaf and pat into and up sides of pan to form a rim. Bake for 5 to 6 minutes. Evenly spread tomato sauce over partially baked crust. Sprinkle Italian seasoning over sauce. Layer browned meat, onion, green pepper, olives, and mushrooms over sauce. Evenly sprinkle Cheddar and mozzarella cheese over top. Bake for 20 to 25 minutes or until crust is browned. Place baking sheet on a wire rack and let set for 5 minutes. Cut into 8 servings.

Each serving equals:

HE: 2½ Protein • 1¼ Vegetable • 1 Bread • ¼ Fat

259 Calories • 9 gm Fat • 20 gm Protein •
22 gm Carbohydrate • 840 mg Sodium •
150 mg Calcium • 2 gm Fiber

DIABETIC: 2 Meat • 1 Vegetable • 1 Starch • ½ Fat

"Sausage" Strata Casserole

If your desire for a healthier lifestyle or maybe doctor's orders have driven sausage from your table, here's a great way to enjoy the traditional flavor you love without sacrificing your health! You'll discover it's all in the spices blended into this old-fashioned dish that arrives at the table beautifully golden-brown and absolutely irresistible!

● Serves 6

> 6 slices reduced-calorie white or Italian bread, cut into 1-inch cubes
>
> 8 ounces ground 90% lean turkey or beef
>
> ½ teaspoon poultry seasoning
>
> ¼ teaspoon ground sage
>
> ¼ teaspoon garlic powder
>
> ¾ cup Yoplait plain fat-free yogurt
>
> ⅓ cup Carnation Nonfat Dry Milk Powder
>
> 1 teaspoon cornstarch
>
> 3 eggs or equivalent in egg substitute
>
> ½ cup (one 2.5-ounce jar) sliced mushrooms, drained
>
> ¼ cup sliced green onion
>
> 1 teaspoon prepared mustard
>
> ⅛ teaspoon black pepper
>
> ⅓ cup (1½ ounces) shredded Kraft reduced-fat Cheddar cheese

Preheat oven to 350 degrees. Spray an 8-by-8-inch baking dish with butter-flavored cooking spray. Evenly arrange bread cubes in prepared baking dish. In a large skillet sprayed with butter-flavored cooking spray, brown meat. Stir in poultry seasoning, sage, and garlic powder. In a large bowl, combine yogurt, dry milk powder, cornstarch, and eggs. Add mushrooms, green onion, mustard, and black pepper. Mix gently to combine. Stir in browned meat mixture. Pour over bread cubes. Bake for 30 to 35 minutes. Sprinkle Cheddar cheese evenly over top. Continue baking for 10 to 15 minutes or until center is firm and cheese melts. Place baking dish on a wire rack and let set for 5 minutes. Cut into 6 servings.

Each serving equals:

HE: 1½ Protein (½ limited) • ½ Bread •
⅓ Skim Milk • ¼ Vegetable

---

191 Calories • 7 gm Fat • 17 gm Protein •
15 gm Carbohydrate • 339 mg Sodium •
152 mg Calcium • 3 gm Fiber

DIABETIC: 1½ Meat • 1 Starch/Carbohydrate

Creamy Baked Tacos

Mexican food is always a terrific choice when you're cutting a few culinary corners, because it's so high in flavor, you feel satisfied! These "soft" tacos are simple to fix, and while they're baking, you can watch the news and just relax before dinner. ☻ Serves 6

> 8 ounces ground 90% lean turkey or beef
> ½ cup water
> 1 tablespoon taco seasoning
> 6 (6-inch) flour tortillas
> ¾ cup (3 ounces) shredded Kraft reduced-fat Cheddar cheese
> 1 (10¾-ounce) can Healthy Request Cream of Mushroom Soup
> ⅓ cup skim milk
> 2 cups finely shredded lettuce
> 1 cup finely chopped fresh tomato
> 6 tablespoons Land O Lakes no-fat sour cream

Preheat oven to 325 degrees. Spray an 8-by-8-inch baking dish with olive oil–flavored cooking spray. In a large skillet sprayed with olive oil–flavored cooking spray, brown meat. Stir in water and taco seasoning. Bring mixture to a boil. Lower heat and simmer for 10 minutes, stirring occasionally. Evenly spoon about ¼ cup meat mixture onto each tortilla. Roll tortillas and place in prepared baking dish, seam side down. Evenly sprinkle Cheddar cheese over top. In a small bowl, combine mushroom soup and milk. Pour mixture evenly over top of tortillas. Bake for 30 to 35 minutes. For each serving, place 1 tortilla on plate, sprinkle ⅓ cup lettuce and full 2 tablespoons tomato over top, and garnish with 1 tablespoon sour cream.

Each serving equals:

HE: 1⅔ Protein • 1 Bread • 1 Vegetable • ½ Slider •
8 Optional Calories

232 Calories • 8 gm Fat • 15 gm Protein •
25 gm Carbohydrate • 552 mg Sodium •
183 mg Calcium • 1 gm Fiber

DIABETIC: 1½ Meat • 1½ Starch/Carbohydrate •
½ Vegetable

Faux Steak with Green Pepper Sauce

Some fancy restaurants serve steak with a tangy pepper sauce, but I'm just not willing to blow the month's food budget on a big chunk of beef. Here's a version that will tantalize your taste buds and appeal to your eyes as well. Only your pocketbook will know for sure!

❍ Serves 6

> 16 ounces ground 90% lean turkey or beef
> 1/8 teaspoon black pepper
> 6 tablespoons (1 1/2 ounces) dried fine bread crumbs
> 1 3/4 cups (one 15-ounce can) Hunt's Chunky Tomato Sauce☆
> 1/2 cup sliced onion
> 2 cups coarsely chopped green bell peppers
> 1 teaspoon prepared mustard
> 2 teaspoons Worcestershire sauce
> 1 tablespoon Brown Sugar Twin

In a large bowl, combine meat, black pepper, bread crumbs, and 1/4 cup tomato sauce. Mix well to combine. Using a 1/3 cup measure as a guide, form into 6 patties. Place patties in a large skillet sprayed with butter-flavored cooking spray. Brown patties for 3 minutes on both sides. Sprinkle onion and green pepper over browned patties. Continue cooking for 4 to 5 minutes. In a small bowl, combine mustard, Worcestershire sauce, Brown Sugar Twin, and remaining 1 1/2 cups tomato sauce. Pour sauce mixture evenly over top. Lower heat, cover, and simmer for 15 minutes. When serving, evenly spoon sauce over patties.

Each serving equals:

HE: 2 Protein • 2 Vegetable • ⅓ Bread •
1 Optional Calorie

---

167 Calories • 7 gm Fat • 15 gm Protein •
11 gm Carbohydrate • 622 mg Sodium •
21 mg Calcium • 2 gm Fiber

DIABETIC: 2 Meat • 2 Vegetable
or 2 Meat • ½ Starch/Carbohydrate

Chunky Stew Pot Pie

Sometimes the best kind of thrift is not having to throw out leftovers that sat in the fridge too long! This tasty, biscuit-topped meat and veggies delight makes great use of just a little roast beef—and is delicious enough to serve to your friends. ◐ Serves 6

> 1 cup chopped celery
> 1½ cups sliced carrots
> ½ cup chopped onion
> ¼ cup water
> 1½ cups (8 ounces) diced lean cooked roast beef
> ½ cup frozen peas, thawed
> 1 (12-ounce) jar Heinz Fat Free Beef Gravy
> 1½ tablespoons dried fine bread crumbs
> 1 teaspoon dried parsley flakes
> ½ teaspoon paprika
> 1 (7.5-ounce) can Pillsbury refrigerated buttermilk biscuits

Place celery, carrots, onion, and water in an 8-by-8-inch glass baking dish. Cover and microwave on HIGH (100% power) for 6 to 8 minutes or until vegetables are tender. Stir in roast beef, peas, and gravy. Re-cover and microwave on HIGH for 3 to 4 minutes. Mix well. In a small bowl, combine bread crumbs, parsley flakes, and paprika. Separate biscuits and cut each into 3 pieces. Evenly drop biscuit pieces over top of stew mixture. Lightly spray biscuit pieces with butter-flavored cooking spray. Sprinkle bread crumb mixture evenly over top. Microwave on HIGH, uncovered, 3 to 4 minutes or until biscuits spring back when lightly touched. Place baking dish on a wire rack and let set for 5 minutes. Cut into 6 servings.

HINTS: 1. If you don't have leftovers, purchase a chunk of lean cooked roast beef from your local deli.

2. Thaw peas by placing in a colander and rinsing under hot water for one minute.

Each serving equals:

HE: 1½ Bread • 1⅓ Protein • 1 Vegetable •
¼ Slider • 5 Optional Calories

204 Calories • 4 gm Fat • 16 gm Protein •
26 gm Carbohydrate • 707 mg Sodium •
30 mg Calcium • 3 gm Fiber

DIABETIC: 1½ Starch • 1 Meat • ½ Vegetable

Nacho Squares

Here's another easy make-at-home Mexican dish that's a true man-pleaser! (I tested it on my truck drivin' man, and Cliff said, "Thumbs up!") I think the topping on these is so much tastier than the kind you get in restaurants, and without all that extra fat, there's just good-for-you goodness piled high!   ☻   Serves 8

> 8 ounces ground 90% lean turkey or beef
> 1 cup chopped green bell pepper
> ½ cup chopped onion
> 1¾ cups (one 15-ounce can) Hunt's Chunky Tomato Sauce
> 6 ounces (one 8-ounce can) red kidney beans, drained and slightly
>   mashed
> 1 tablespoon taco seasoning
> 1 (8-ounce) can Pillsbury Reduced Fat Crescent Rolls
> ⅔ cup (2¼ ounces) shredded Kraft reduced-fat Cheddar cheese

Preheat oven to 415 degrees. In a large skillet sprayed with olive oil–flavored cooking spray, brown meat, green pepper, and onion. Add tomato sauce, kidney beans, and taco seasoning. Mix well to combine. Lower heat and simmer, stirring occasionally. Meanwhile, pat rolls into an ungreased 10-by-15-inch baking sheet. Gently press dough to cover bottom of pan, being sure to seal perforations. Bake for 5 to 7 minutes or until lightly browned. Spread hot meat mixture over crust and continue baking for 10 minutes. Evenly sprinkle Cheddar cheese over top and continue baking 5 minutes or until cheese melts. Place baking sheet on a wire rack and let set for 5 minutes. Cut into 8 servings.

HINT: Do not use inexpensive rolls as they don't cover the pan properly.

Each serving equals:

HE: 1½ Protein • 1¼ Vegetable • 1 Bread

---

200 Calories • 8 gm Fat • 12 gm Protein • 20 gm Carbohydrate • 674 mg Sodium • 61 mg Calcium • 2 gm Fiber

---

DIABETIC: 1 Meat • 1 Vegetable • 1 Starch

Skillet Hash

It's not a bit fancy, but it sure is good—that's what everyone who sampled this hurry-up hash told me, and I agree! This is a great Sunday supper dish, and would even be a welcome treat at a weekend brunch, so give it a try soon!   ☻   Serves 4 (1 full cup)

> 1½ cups (8 ounces) diced cooked lean roast beef
> 3 full cups (16 ounces) finely chopped cooked potatoes
> 1 cup chopped onion
> 2 teaspoons dried parsley flakes
> ⅛ teaspoon black pepper
> 1 cup skim milk

In a medium bowl, combine beef, potatoes, onion, parsley flakes, and black pepper. In a medium skillet sprayed with butter-flavored cooking spray, spread mixture evenly over bottom. Cook over medium heat for 15 minutes, or until bottom browns, without stirring. Add skim milk. Mix well to combine. Lower heat, and simmer for 15 minutes or until most of the liquid is absorbed and potatoes are crisp.

Each serving equals:

HE: 2 Protein • 1 Bread • ½ Vegetable • ¼ Skim Milk

236 Calories • 4 gm Fat • 21 gm Protein •
29 gm Carbohydrate • 74 mg Sodium •
92 mg Calcium • 3 gm Fiber

DIABETIC: 2 Meat • 1½ Starch/Carbohydrate

Pork

If you've been staying away from pork because you thought it packed too much fat, it's time to celebrate "the other white meat" with these super-satisfying dishes that are full of flavor, not calories! Why not dazzle your loved ones tonight with Simmered Grande Pork Tenders or Harvest Time Pork Casserole? Their smiles will quickly tell you that these recipes are oh-so-scrumptious!

Pork

Author's Note: Some of these recipes call for lean cooked roast pork, but if you haven't got leftovers, purchase a chunk at your local deli. If you do cook the pork yourself, be careful not to overbrown it or it will become tough.

Simmered Grande Pork Tenders

Cliff loves pork, and now that we can purchase lean cuts everywhere, I am serving it more often. This is a perfect example of simple preparation that makes for a spectacular meal. Served with a baked potato and some fresh green beans, this makes a terrific company dish. ☻ Serves 4

> 4 (4-ounce) lean tenderized pork tenderloins or cutlets
> 1¾ cups (one 15-ounce can) Hunt's Chunky Tomato Sauce
> ½ cup (one 2.5-ounce jar) sliced mushrooms, undrained
> 1 teaspoon chili seasoning
> ¼ teaspoon dried minced garlic
> 1 tablespoon Brown Sugar Twin

In a large skillet sprayed with olive oil–flavored cooking spray, lightly brown meat on both sides. In a medium bowl, combine tomato sauce, undrained mushrooms, chili seasoning, garlic, and Brown Sugar Twin. Evenly pour mixture over browned meat. Lower heat, cover, and simmer for 20 minutes. Uncover and continue simmering for 10 minutes, or until meat is tender. When serving, evenly spoon sauce over meat.

Each serving equals:

HE: 3 Protein • 2 Vegetable • 1 Optional Calorie

182 Calories • 6 gm Fat • 26 gm Protein •
6 gm Carbohydrate • 858 mg Sodium •
26 mg Calcium • 2 gm Fiber

DIABETIC: 3 Meat • 2 Vegetable

Pork and Green Beans Supreme

This wonderfully creamy dish is a kind of pork stroganoff and tastes as if you really splurged—when you didn't have to! Some people recommend pounding the pork tenderloins to make them even more tender, but I don't find it necessary as long as you don't try to cook this dish too quickly. ● Serves 6 (1 cup)

> *16 ounces lean pork tenderloin or steak, cut into 36 pieces*
> *2 cups (one 16-ounce can) cut green beans, rinsed and drained*
> *3 cups hot cooked noodles, rinsed and drained*
> *1 (10¾-ounce) can Healthy Request Cream of Mushroom Soup*
> *¼ cup skim milk*
> *¼ cup Land O Lakes no-fat sour cream*
> *1 teaspoon chili seasoning*
> *¼ teaspoon black pepper*

In a large skillet sprayed with butter-flavored cooking spray, brown meat. Stir in green beans and noodles. Add mushroom soup, skim milk, sour cream, chili seasoning, and black pepper. Mix well to combine. Lower heat, cover, and simmer for 10 minutes, or until mixture is heated through, stirring occasionally.

HINT: 2½ cups uncooked noodles usually cooks to about 3 cups.

Each serving equals:

HE: 2 Protein • 1 Bread • ⅔ Vegetable • ½ Slider • 2 Optional Calories

---

254 Calories • 6 gm Fat • 22 gm Protein • 28 gm Carbohydrate • 275 mg Sodium • 94 mg Calcium • 2 gm Fiber

---

DIABETIC: 2 Meat • 1½ Starch • ½ Vegetable

Roast Pork with Potato Dumplings and Kraut

I've become a real fan of making fast potato dumplings with instant potatoes—you save so much time and money, and they taste absolutely delicious! Spiced with my favorite sauerkraut, this pork dish is truly "budget gourmet"! ☺ Serves 4

> 2 cups (10 ounces) diced lean cooked roast pork
> 3½ cups (two 14½-ounce cans) Frank's Bavarian-style sauerkraut, drained
> ⅔ cup (2 ounces) instant potato flakes
> ¾ cup all-purpose flour
> 1½ teaspoons baking powder
> 2 teaspoons dried parsley flakes
> ⅓ cup Carnation Nonfat Dry Milk Powder
> ⅓ cup water
> 1 egg or equivalent in egg substitute

In a large saucepan, combine pork and sauerkraut. Cover and cook over medium heat for 10 minutes, stirring occasionally. Meanwhile, in a large bowl, combine potato flakes, flour, baking powder, parsley flakes, dry milk powder, water, and egg. Mix well to combine. Let set for 3 minutes. Using a ¼ cup measuring cup as a guide, drop batter into hot sauerkraut mixture to form 4 dumplings. Re-cover and continue cooking for 10 minutes, or until dumplings are firm. For each serving, place 1 dumpling on a plate and spoon about 1 full cup sauerkraut mixture over top.

HINT: If you can't find Bavarian sauerkraut, use regular sauerkraut, ½ teaspoon caraway seeds, and 1 teaspoon Brown Sugar Twin.

Each serving equals:

HE: 2¾ Protein (¼ limited) • 1¾ Vegetable • 1½ Bread • ¼ Skim Milk

285 Calories • 5 gm Fat • 24 gm Protein • 36 gm Carbohydrate • 1,650 mg Sodium • 263 mg Calcium • 7 gm Fiber

DIABETIC: 3 Meat • 2 Vegetable • 1½ Starch

Pork with Kidney Beans and Macaroni

If you've been looking to increase the amount of fiber in your diet, here's a dish you'll want to serve often! It's a tummy-warming treat the whole family will love, and you didn't have to go into debt to bring it to the table. ○ Serves 4 (1½ cups)

> *10 ounces (one 16-ounce can) kidney beans, rinsed and drained*
> *1 cup (5 ounces) diced lean cooked roast pork*
> *½ cup chopped onion*
> *1 cup shredded carrots*
> *1¾ cups (one 15-ounce can) Hunt's Chunky Tomato Sauce*
> *2 cups hot cooked shell macaroni, rinsed and drained*
> *1 teaspoon dried parsley flakes*

In a large skillet sprayed with butter-flavored cooking spray, combine kidney beans, pork, onion, carrots, and tomato sauce. Bring mixture to a boil. Lower heat, cover and simmer for 15 minutes or until carrots and onion are tender. Add macaroni and parsley flakes. Mix gently to combine. Continue simmering for 5 minutes, or until mixture is heated through, stirring occasionally.

HINT: 1⅓ cups uncooked macaroni usually cooks to about 2 cups.

Each serving equals:

HE: 2½ Protein • 2½ Vegetable • 1 Bread

---

242 Calories • 2 gm Fat • 15 gm Protein •
41 gm Carbohydrate • 1,079 mg Sodium •
37 mg Calcium • 8 gm Fiber

DIABETIC: 2 Meat • 2 Vegetable • 2 Starch

Harvest Time Pork Casserole

Here's a dish so gorgeously golden, you'll be tempted to dig right in instead of waiting a few minutes for it to set! As the creamy, cheesy sauce bubbles away in your oven, don't be surprised to find everyone already at the table before dinner is announced.   ☻   Serves 4

> 2 cups hot cooked elbow macaroni, rinsed and drained
> 2 cups (one 16-ounce can) cut green beans, rinsed and drained
> ¼ cup finely chopped onion
> 1¾ cups (one 14½-ounce can) Frank's Bavarian-style sauerkraut, drained
> 1½ cups (8 ounces) diced lean cooked roast pork
> 1 (10¾-ounce) can Healthy Request Cream of Mushroom Soup
> ¼ cup skim milk
> 4 (¾-ounce) slices Kraft reduced-fat Swiss cheese

Preheat oven to 350 degrees. Spray an 8-by-8-inch baking dish with butter-flavored cooking spray. In a large bowl, combine macaroni, green beans, onion, sauerkraut, and roast pork. Add mushroom soup and skim milk. Mix well to combine. Spread mixture into prepared baking dish. Bake for 30 minutes. Evenly arrange Swiss cheese slices over top. Continue baking for 10 minutes or until cheese melts. Place baking dish on a wire rack and let set for 5 minutes. Divide into 4 servings.

HINT: If you can't find Bavarian sauerkraut, use regular sauerkraut, ½ teaspoon caraway seeds, and 1 teaspoon Brown Sugar Twin.

Each serving equals:

HE: 3 Protein • 2 Vegetable • 1 Bread • ½ Slider • 7 Optional Calories

---

298 Calories • 6 gm Fat • 25 gm Protein • 36 gm Carbohydrate • 1,085 mg Sodium • 340 mg Calcium • 4 gm Fiber

---

DIABETIC: 3 Meat • 2 Vegetable • 1½ Starch

Ham

You might not recall that ham used to be considered a real luxury, unless you lived on a farm and could cure your own! Now this everyday favorite is readily available and in healthy versions, so you can enjoy it whenever you like. I suggest going for the gusto with my Ham with Polynesian Peach Sauce, or perhaps celebrating anytime with Holiday Ham with Cranberry Raisin Sauce. They're truly terrific!

Ham

Macaroni and Cheese Extraordinaire

This all-American family favorite is a standard budget entree, but why settle for "standard" when you can have superb? Creamier and cheesier, tangier and tastier—here's a macaroni and cheese that gives you more, more, and more of what you love!

❂ Serves 6 (1 cup)

> ¼ cup chopped onion
> 3 cups hot cooked elbow macaroni, rinsed and drained
> 1 full cup (6 ounces) diced Dubuque 97% fat-free ham or any extra-lean ham
> 1¾ cups (one 14 ½-ounce can) stewed tomatoes, undrained
> 1½ cups (6 ounces) shredded Kraft reduced-fat Cheddar cheese
> 1 (10¾-ounce) can Healthy Request Cream of Mushroom Soup

In a large skillet sprayed with butter-flavored cooking spray, sauté onion for 5 minutes or just until tender. Stir in macaroni, ham, undrained stewed tomatoes, and Cheddar cheese. Add mushroom soup. Mix well to combine. Lower heat, cover, and simmer for 15 minutes, or until mixture is heated through, stirring occasionally.

HINT: 2 cups uncooked elbow macaroni usually cooks to about 3 cups.

Each serving equals:

HE: 2 Protein • 1 Bread • ⅔ Vegetable • ¼ Slider • 8 Optional Calories

260 Calories • 8 gm Fat • 17 gm Protein • 30 gm Carbohydrate • 911 mg Sodium • 280 mg Calcium • 2 gm Fiber

DIABETIC: 1½ Meat • 1 Starch • 1 Vegetable

Ham and Potato Skillet Hash

This savory ham hash is another terrific choice for brunch or Sunday supper. It's a favorite at our house because of the green beans (Cliff's best-loved veggie), but it's high on my list, too, because it's so creamy and rich! ♥ Serves 4 (1 full cup)

1½ cups (9 ounces) diced Dubuque 97% fat-free ham or any extra-lean ham
2 full cups (12 ounces) diced cooked potatoes
½ cup chopped onion
2 cups (one 16-ounce can) cut green beans, rinsed and drained
1 (10¾-ounce) can Healthy Request Cream of Mushroom Soup
1 teaspoon dried parsley flakes
⅛ teaspoon black pepper

In a large skillet sprayed with butter-flavored cooking spray, sauté ham, potatoes, and onion for 5 minutes. Add green beans, mushroom soup, parsley flakes, and black pepper. Mix well to combine. Lower heat and simmer for 10 minutes, or until mixture is heated through, stirring occasionally.

Each serving equals:

HE: 1½ Protein • 1¼ Vegetable • ¾ Bread •
½ Slider • 1 Optional Calorie

176 Calories • 4 gm Fat • 13 gm Protein •
22 gm Carbohydrate • 846 mg Sodium •
76 mg Calcium • 2 gm Fiber

DIABETIC: 2 Meat • 1 Vegetable • 1 Starch

Creamy Potatoes and Ham

Scalloped potatoes are a classic Midwestern delight, and recipes like this one are often handed down from mother to daughter over the years. This one doesn't have a long history the way some do, but it tastes like it does! ☉ Serves 6

4 cups (20 ounces) diced raw potatoes

1½ cups (9 ounces) diced Dubuque 97% fat-free ham or any
    extra-lean ham

¾ cup finely chopped onion

⅔ cup Carnation Nonfat Dry Milk Powder

½ cup water

1 (10¾-ounce) can Healthy Request Cream of Mushroom Soup

1 teaspoon prepared mustard

1 teaspoon dried parsley flakes

¼ teaspoon black pepper

¼ teaspoon paprika

Preheat oven to 375 degrees. Spray an 8-by-8-inch baking dish with butter-flavored cooking spray. Layer half of potatoes, ham, and onion in prepared baking dish. Repeat layers. In a small bowl, combine dry milk powder, water, mushroom soup, mustard, parsley flakes, and black pepper. Pour mixture evenly over potatoes. Evenly sprinkle paprika over top. Cover and bake for 45 minutes. Remove cover and continue baking for 30 minutes, or until potatoes are tender. Place baking dish on a wire rack and let set for 5 minutes. Cut into 6 servings.

Each serving equals:

HE: 1 Protein • ⅔ Bread • ⅓ Skim Milk •
¼ Vegetable • ¼ Slider • 8 Optional Calories

167 Calories • 3 gm Fat • 12 gm Protein •
23 gm Carbohydrate • 617 mg Sodium •
138 mg Calcium • 1 gm Fiber

DIABETIC: 1½ Starch/Carbohydrate • 1 Meat

Ham with Polynesian Peach Sauce

Ham is just the perfect meat for serving with a sweet sauce like this tropical pleaser! You don't have to hop a plane to feel the sultry warmth of the islands, just take a bite of this succulent delight— and you're there in spirit! ☻ Serves 4

4 (3-ounce) slices Dubuque 97% fat-free ham or any extra-lean ham
¾ cup chopped green bell pepper
¼ cup chopped green onions
2 cups (one 16-ounce can) sliced peaches, packed in fruit juice,
    drained, and ⅓ cup liquid reserved
2 tablespoons Brown Sugar Twin
1 teaspoon cornstarch
1 tablespoon Heinz Light Harvest Ketchup or any reduced-sodium
    ketchup
1 teaspoon lemon juice

In a large skillet sprayed with butter-flavored cooking spray, lightly brown ham on both sides. Lower heat. Meanwhile, in a medium skillet sprayed with butter-flavored cooking spray, sauté green pepper and onion for 5 minutes or just until tender. In a small bowl, combine reserved peach liquid, Brown Sugar Twin, and cornstarch. Stir mixture into vegetables. Continue cooking until mixture thickens, stirring often. Add ketchup, lemon juice, and peaches. Mix gently to combine. Continue cooking for 5 minutes or until peaches are heated through, stirring occasionally. For each serving, place a slice of ham on a plate and spoon about ½ cup peach sauce over top.

HINT: A 3-ounce slice is usually about ⅓-inch thick.

Each serving equals:

HE: 2 Protein • 1 Fruit • ½ Vegetable •
10 Optional Calories

191 Calories • 3 gm Fat • 15 gm Protein •
26 gm Carbohydrate • 729 mg Sodium •
25 mg Calcium • 3 gm Fiber

DIABETIC: 2 Meat • 1 Fruit • ½ Starch/Carbohydrate

Holiday Ham with Cranberry Raisin Sauce

I think this would be just delightful as the centerpiece at a Christmas morning brunch! It's fantastically festive, it'll fill the house with a luscious fragrance while it's cooking, and even the color suggests it's time for your mouth to make merry!　●　Serves 4

> 4 (3-ounce) slices Dubuque 97% fat-free ham or any extra-lean ham
>
> 1 (4-serving) package JELL-O sugar-free vanilla cook-and-serve pudding mix
>
> 1 cup Ocean Spray reduced-calorie cranberry juice cocktail
>
> 1/4 teaspoon ground cinnamon
>
> 6 tablespoons raisins

In a large skillet sprayed with butter-flavored cooking spray, lightly brown ham on both sides. Lower heat. Meanwhile, in a medium saucepan, combine dry pudding mix and Cranapple beverage drink. Stir in cinnamon and raisins. Cook over medium heat until mixture thickens and starts to boil, stirring constantly. Remove from heat. For each serving, place 1 slice of ham on a plate and spoon a full 1/4 cup sauce over top.

HINT:　A 3-ounce slice of ham is usually 1/3 inch thick.

Each serving equals:

HE: 2 Protein • 3/4 Fruit • 1/4 Slider

---

167 Calories • 3 gm Fat • 14 gm Protein •
21 gm Carbohydrate • 845 mg Sodium •
8 mg Calcium • 0 gm Fiber

DIABETIC: 2 Meat • 1 Fruit

Ham and Broccoli Garden Skillet

Lean ham has transformed our expectations about what meats we can enjoy as part of a healthy lifestyle. We used to think of ham as an occasional treat, but now it can be stirred into tasty everyday dishes like this smooth skillet supper that makes it a star!

● Serves 4 (1 cup)

> 1 full cup (6 ounces) diced Dubuque 97% fat-free or any extra-lean ham
> 1/2 cup chopped onion
> 1 cup finely shredded carrots
> 1 cup (one 8-ounce can) cream-style corn
> 1 (10¾-ounce) can Healthy Request Cream of Broccoli Soup
> 1½ cups hot cooked noodles, rinsed and drained
> ¼ teaspoon black pepper
> 1 teaspoon dried parsley flakes

In a large skillet sprayed with butter-flavored cooking spray, sauté ham, onion, and carrots for about 5 minutes. Stir in corn and broccoli soup. Add noodles, black pepper, and parsley flakes. Mix well to combine. Lower heat and simmer for 10 minutes, or until mixture is heated through, stirring occasionally.

HINT: 1¼ cups uncooked noodles usually cooks to about 1½ cups.

Each serving equals:

> HE: 1¼ Bread • 1 Protein • ¾ Vegetable • ½ Slider • 1 Optional Calorie
>
> ---
> 259 Calories • 7 gm Fat • 14 gm Protein • 35 gm Carbohydrate • 796 mg Sodium • 103 mg Calcium • 3 gm Fiber
>
> ---
> DIABETIC: 2 Starch/Carbohydrate • 1 Meat • 1 Fat • ½ Vegetable

Mexicali Ham Bake

You'll never believe just how delicious this spicy-tangy blend of flavors will be until you cut into its crust after baking—and the aroma fills your kitchen! This freezes beautifully, so even if you live alone or cook just for two, the extra servings will heat up whenever you want to serve them. ☯ Serves 4

> ¾ cup Bisquick Reduced Fat Baking Mix
> ¾ cup chunky salsa (mild, medium, or hot)
> ¼ cup chopped onion
> 1 full cup (6 ounces) diced Dubuque 97% fat-free ham or any
>   extra-lean ham
> 2 cups (one 16-ounce can) cut green beans, rinsed and drained
> 1 teaspoon dried parsley flakes
> ¾ cup (3 ounces) shredded Kraft reduced-fat Cheddar cheese

Preheat oven to 350 degrees. Spray an 8-by-8-inch baking dish with butter-flavored cooking spray. In a medium bowl, combine baking mix and salsa. Add onion, ham, green beans, and parsley flakes. Mix well to combine. Spread mixture into prepared baking dish. Evenly sprinkle Cheddar cheese over top. Bake for 45 to 50 minutes. Place baking dish on a wire rack and let set for 5 minutes. Cut into 4 servings.

Each serving equals:

HE: 2½ Vegetable • 2 Protein • 1 Bread

211 Calories • 7 gm Fat • 15 gm Protein •
22 gm Carbohydrate • 968 mg Sodium •
270 mg Calcium • 1 gm Fiber

DIABETIC: 2 Vegetable • 2 Meat • 1 Starch

Brunch Cornbread-Ham Casserole

What could be more cozy than sitting down to brunch with friends and serving up this scrumptious baked dish? The ingredients are somewhat unusual, it's true, but combining them is the key to a mouthwatering meal not soon forgotten! ❍ Serves 4

½ cup (3 ounces) yellow cornmeal

1 teaspoon baking powder

½ cup Yoplait plain fat-free yogurt

⅓ cup Kraft fat-free mayonnaise

¼ cup Cary's Sugar Free Maple Syrup

¾ cup (3 ounces) grated Kraft reduced-fat Cheddar cheese

1 full cup (6 ounces) diced Dubuque 97% fat-free ham or any
    extra-lean ham

2 cups (one 16-ounce can) cut green beans, rinsed and drained

Preheat oven to 400 degrees. Spray an 8-by-8-inch baking dish with butter-flavored cooking spray. In a medium bowl, combine cornmeal and baking powder. Stir in yogurt, mayonnaise, and maple syrup. Add Cheddar cheese, ham, and green beans. Mix well to combine. Pour mixture into prepared baking dish. Bake for 30 to 40 minutes or until lightly browned. Place baking dish on a wire rack and let set for 5 minutes. Cut into 4 pieces.

HINT: Good served with additional Cary's Sugar Free Maple Syrup drizzled on top, but don't forget to count the few additional calories.

Each serving equals:

HE: 2 Protein • 1 Bread • 1 Vegetable • ½ Slider •
12 Optional Calories

244 Calories • 8 gm Fat • 17 gm Protein •
26 gm Carbohydrate • 870 mg Sodium •
308 mg Calcium • 2 gm Fiber

DIABETIC: 2 Meats • 1½ Starch • 1 Vegetable

Swiss Ham and Biscuit Bake

Here's another truly delightful entree that makes lunch something luscious and brunch better than you dreamed! It's crusty and creamy, and surprisingly easy to prepare, so instead of serving up the same old ham and Swiss on rye, mix up something special that really feeds the soul! ○ Serves 4

> 1 full cup (6 ounces) diced Dubuque 97% fat-free ham or any
>   extra-lean ham
> ½ cup frozen peas, thawed
> ½ cup (one 2.5-ounce jar) sliced mushrooms, undrained
> 1 (10¾-ounce) can Healthy Request Cream of Celery Soup
> ⅔ cup Carnation Nonfat Dry Milk Powder
> 1¼ cups water
> ¾ cup Bisquick Reduced Fat Baking Mix
> 1 teaspoon dried parsley flakes
> 2 (¾-ounce) slices Kraft reduced-fat Swiss cheese, shredded
> 1 teaspoon prepared mustard

Preheat oven to 400 degrees. Spray an 8-by-8-inch baking dish with butter-flavored cooking spray. In a large skillet, sprayed with butter-flavored cooking spray, combine ham, peas, undrained mushrooms, and celery soup. Cook over medium heat for 5 minutes, stirring occasionally. Meanwhile in a small bowl, combine dry milk powder and water. Pour ¾ cup of milk mixture into skillet with ham. Mix well to combine. Lower heat and simmer while preparing biscuits. In a medium bowl, combine baking mix, parsley flakes, and Swiss cheese. Stir in remaining ½ cup milk mixture and mustard. Mix just to combine. Pour ham mixture into prepared baking dish. Using a large tablespoon as a guide, evenly drop batter onto ham mixture to form 4 biscuits. Bake for 15 to 18 minutes. Place baking dish on a wire rack and let set for 5 minutes. Divide into 4 servings.

HINT: Thaw peas by placing in a colander and rinsing under hot water for one minute.

Each serving equals:

HE: 1½ Protein • 1¼ Bread • ½ Skim Milk •
¼ Vegetable • ½ Slider • 1 Optional Calorie

254 Calories • 6 gm Fat • 17 gm Protein •
33 gm Carbohydrate • 1,169 mg Sodium •
283 mg Calcium • 2 gm Fiber

DIABETIC: 2 Starch/Carbohydrate • 1 Meat

Ham 'n' Tortilla Roll-Ups

Perfect for lunch on the run, these handy "wrapped" sandwiches will surprise you! Mixing cream cheese and salsa may seem an unusual choice, but when that tangy blends "hugs" the sliced ham, you'll think it's gotta be love! ● Serves 4

¼ cup (2 ounces) Philadelphia fat-free cream cheese
½ cup chunky salsa (mild, medium, or hot)
4 (6-inch) flour tortillas
1 cup (6 ounces) Healthy Choice deli sliced 97% fat-free ham or
  any extra-lean ham
½ cup finely shredded lettuce

In a small bowl, stir cream cheese with a spoon until soft. Add salsa. Mix well to combine. Spread about 3 tablespoons cream cheese mixture over each tortilla. Evenly divide ham slices and arrange over tortillas. Sprinkle 2 tablespoons lettuce over top of each. Roll up and wrap each tightly in aluminum foil. Refrigerate for at least 30 minutes.

Each serving equals:

HE: 1¼ Protein • 1 Bread • ½ Vegetable

170 Calories • 6 gm Fat • 12 gm Protein •
17 gm Carbohydrate • 938 mg Sodium •
51 mg Calcium • 0 gm Fiber

DIABETIC: 1 Meat • 1 Starch • 1 Vegetable

This and That

I like to say that hot dogs, corned beef, and even pastrami, that former "no-no," have all gone to reform school—and now provide wonderful choices whether you're concerned about nutrition, cost, or both! Dazzle your kids with Fantastic Frankfurter Tetrazzini, or win your husband's heart when you serve up Pastrami Pizza Potatoes—they'll help you cut costs without trimming any of the flavor!

This and That

Crock Pot Corned Beef and Cabbage

Here's a dish to celebrate my Irish heritage, for what self-respecting Irishwoman could offer you her best thrifty recipes without including one for this St. Paddy's Day classic? If you've been skipping this favorite in order to trim the fat in your diet, welcome back!

○ Serves 6 (1½ cups)

> 2½ cups thinly sliced carrots
> 1 cup chopped onion
> 4 cups coarsely chopped cabbage
> 3 cups (15 ounces) diced raw potatoes
> 1 cup water
> 3 (2.5-ounce) packages Carl Buddig 90% lean corned beef,
>   shredded

In a slow cooker container, combine carrots, onion, cabbage, and potatoes. Add water. Mix well to combine. Stir in corned beef. Cover and cook on LOW for 6 to 8 hours. Mix well just before serving.

Each serving equals:

HE: 2½ Vegetable • 1¼ Protein • ½ Bread

131 Calories • 3 gm Fat • 9 gm Protein •
17 gm Carbohydrate • 512 mg Sodium •
47 mg Calcium • 3 gm Fiber

DIABETIC: 1 Vegetable • 1 Meat • 1 Starch

Corned Beef and Bavarian Kraut Casserole

I wanted to see what other tasty possibilities I could create with lean corned beef, and stirred up this savory baked dish that does it proud! It bakes up so custardy and rich, your family will celebrate with each bite! ☻ Serves 6

> 1¾ cups (one 14½-ounce can) Frank's Bavarian-style sauerkraut, drained
>
> ¼ cup finely chopped onion
>
> 2 (2.5-ounce) packages Carl Buddig lean corned beef, shredded
>
> ¾ cup Bisquick Reduced Fat Baking Mix
>
> 1 teaspoon dried parsley flakes
>
> ½ cup Kraft fat-free mayonnaise
>
> ⅓ cup skim milk
>
> 1 teaspoon prepared mustard
>
> 3 eggs or equivalent in egg substitute
>
> 4 (¾-ounce) slices Kraft reduced-fat Swiss cheese

Preheat oven to 350 degrees. Spray an 8-by-8-inch baking dish with butter-flavored cooking spray. Evenly spread sauerkraut in prepared baking dish. Sprinkle onion and corned beef evenly over sauerkraut. In a large bowl, combine baking mix, parsley flakes, mayonnaise, skim milk, mustard, and eggs. Mix well using a wire whisk. Pour batter evenly over corned beef. Cut Swiss cheese slices in half diagonally. Evenly arrange cheese pieces over top. Bake for 25 to 30 minutes. Place baking dish on a wire rack and let set for 5 minutes. Cut into 6 servings.

HINT: If you can't find Bavarian sauerkraut, use regular sauerkraut, ½ teaspoon caraway seeds, and 1 teaspoon Brown Sugar Twin.

Each serving equals:

HE: 2 Protein (½ limited) • ⅔ Vegetable • ⅔ Bread •
18 Optional Calories

215 Calories • 9 gm Fat • 13 gm Protein •
18 gm Carbohydrate • 960 mg Sodium •
150 mg Calcium • 1 gm Fiber

DIABETIC: 1½ Meat • 1 Starch/Carbohydrate •
½ Vegetable

Corned Beef and Cabbage with Rice

So many people figure that corned beef and cabbage is a "once-a-year" kind of dish, but now that we can make it healthy, we can make it much more often! This skillet version stirs it up in a creamy new way I think you'll enjoy—Cliff and I surely did!

◐ Serves 4 (1½ cups)

> 1 tablespoon plus 1 teaspoon reduced-calorie margarine
> 5 cups finely shredded cabbage
> ½ cup chopped onion
> 2 (2.5-ounce) packages Carl Buddig 90% lean corned beef, shredded
> 1½ cups hot cooked rice
> ½ cup (one 2.5-ounce jar) sliced mushrooms, drained
> ⅔ cup Carnation Nonfat Dry Milk Powder
> 1½ cups water
> 3 tablespoons all-purpose flour
> ⅓ cup (1½ ounces) shredded Kraft reduced-fat Cheddar cheese

In a large skillet, melt margarine. Stir in cabbage and onion. Sauté for 5 minutes or until vegetables are just tender. Add corned beef, rice, and mushrooms. Mix well to combine. Lower heat and simmer, stirring occasionally. In a covered jar, combine dry milk powder, water and flour. Shake well to blend. Pour milk mixture into cabbage mixture. Stir in Cheddar cheese. Continue simmering for 10 minutes or until mixture thickens and cheese melts, stirring often.

HINT: 1 cup uncooked rice usually cooks to about 1½ cups.

Each serving equals:

HE: 3 Vegetable • 1¾ Protein • 1 Bread • ½ Fat

250 Calories • 6 gm Fat • 18 gm Protein •
31 gm Carbohydrate • 746 mg Sodium •
274 mg Calcium • 3 gm Fiber

DIABETIC: 1½ Meat • 1½ Starch • ½ Skim Milk •
½ Fat • 1 Free Vegetable

Frankfurter-Macaroni Skillet

This mac and cheese combination with sliced franks stirred in is a true kid-pleaser, but if you're planning to serve it to kids under three, make sure you dice the hot dogs instead of slicing them, so they can swallow every bite. My son James would add even more chili sauce to this, but let your own taste buds be the judge.

Serves 4 (1 cup)

> 8 ounces Healthy Choice 97% fat-free frankfurters, sliced
> ⅔ cup Carnation Nonfat Dry Milk Powder
> 1 cup water
> 2 cups hot cooked elbow macaroni, rinsed and drained
> ¾ cup (3 ounces) shredded Kraft reduced-fat Cheddar cheese
> ¼ cup chili sauce
> 1 teaspoon dried onion flakes
> 1 teaspoon dried parsley flakes

In a large skillet sprayed with butter-flavored cooking spray, sauté frankfurters for 5 minutes. In a small bowl, combine dry milk powder and water. Stir milk mixture into skillet with frankfurters. Add macaroni and Cheddar cheese. Mix well to combine. Lower heat and simmer until cheese melts and sauce thickens, stirring often. Stir in chili sauce, onion flakes, and parsley flakes. Continue simmering for 5 minutes, stirring occasionally.

HINT: 1⅓ cups uncooked elbow macaroni usually cooks to about 2 cups.

Each serving equals:

HE: 2⅓ Protein • 1 Bread • ½ Skim Milk •
¼ Slider • 5 Optional Calories

278 Calories • 6 gm Fat • 22 gm Protein •
34 gm Carbohydrate • 851 mg Sodium •
345 mg Calcium • 1 gm Fiber

DIABETIC: 2 Meat • 1½ Starch • ½ Skim Milk *or*
2 Meat • 2 Starch/Carbohydrate

Ballpark Franks

If you'd like to enjoy hot dogs just the way they're served at your favorite stadium, here's my take on this tangy combo. Just warn your kids that if they start to do the "Wave," they'd better not knock over their milk! ☻ Serves 4

4 (2 ounces) Healthy Choice 97% fat-free frankfurters
4 reduced-calorie hot dog buns
1 cup (one 8-ounce can) sauerkraut, drained
2 tablespoons sweet pickle relish
2 tablespoons Heinz Light Harvest Ketchup or any reduced-
    sodium ketchup

Place 1 frankfurter in each bun and arrange buns in an 8-by-8-inch glass baking dish. In a small bowl, combine drained sauerkraut, pickle relish, and ketchup. Spoon full ¼ cup of mixture over top of each frankfurter. Cover and microwave on HIGH (100% power) for 3 to 4 minutes or until heated through.

Each serving equals:

HE: 1⅓ Protein • 1 Bread • ½ Vegetable • ¼ Slider

154 Calories • 2 gm Fat • 9 gm Protein •
25 gm Carbohydrate • 1,066 mg Sodium •
23 mg Calcium • 3 gm Fiber

DIABETIC: 1 Meat • 1 Starch • 1 Vegetable

Fantastic Frankfurter Tetrazzini

Tired of serving turkey tetrazzini, no matter how much your family tells you they like it? Here's a flavorful alternative that has just as much sparkle and fun, but gives the good old hot dog a chance to shine.   ☉   Serves 4 (1 cup)

½ cup chopped onion

8 ounces (½ package) Healthy Choice 97% fat-free frankfurters, diced

1 (10¾-ounce) can Healthy Request Cream of Mushroom Soup

¼ cup skim milk

½ cup (2.5-ounce jar) sliced mushrooms, drained

¾ cup (3 ounces) shredded Kraft reduced-fat Cheddar cheese

2 cups hot cooked spaghetti, rinsed and drained

¼ cup (one 2-ounce jar) chopped pimiento, drained

1 teaspoon dried parsley flakes

¼ teaspoon black pepper

In a large skillet sprayed with butter-flavored cooking spray, sauté onion and frankfurters for 5 minutes. Stir in mushroom soup, skim milk, mushrooms, and Cheddar cheese. Continue cooking for 5 minutes or until cheese melts, stirring often. Add spaghetti, pimiento, parsley flakes, and black pepper. Mix well to combine. Lower heat and simmer 5 minutes or until mixture is heated through, stirring occasionally.

HINT: 1½ cups broken uncooked spaghetti usually cooks to about 2 cups.

Each serving equals:

HE: 2⅓ Protein • 1 Bread • ½ Vegetable • ½ Slider • 7 Optional Calories

283 Calories • 7 gm Fat • 19 gm Protein • 36 gm Carbohydrate • 1,163 mg Sodium • 235 mg Calcium • 2 gm Fiber

DIABETIC: 2 Meat • 2 Starch

Pizza Hot Dog Casserole

I had almost as much fun thinking about this recipe as I did tasting it! There's just something so silly and yet delicious about blending together those two beloved childhood flavors—pizza and hot dogs. Busy moms will love it even more because it's a one-pot dish cooked in the microwave and served straight from the "pot."

☻ Serves 4 (1 cup)

> 8 ounces Healthy Choice 97% fat-free frankfurters, diced
> 1¾ cups (3 ounces) uncooked noodles
> 1¾ cups (one 15-ounce can) Hunt's Chunky Tomato Sauce
> 1 teaspoon pizza seasoning or Italian seasoning
> 1 teaspoon Sugar Twin or Sprinkle Sweet
> ½ cup (one 2.5-ounce jar) sliced mushrooms, undrained
> ⅔ cup (2¼ ounces) shredded Kraft reduced-fat mozzarella cheese

Place frankfurters in an 8-cup glass measuring bowl. Sprinkle uncooked noodles evenly over top. In a medium bowl, combine tomato sauce, pizza seasoning, Sugar Twin, and undrained mushrooms. Pour sauce mixture evenly over noodles. Cover and microwave on HIGH (100% power) for 10 minutes. Stir in mozzarella cheese. Continue microwaving on HIGH for 2 minutes or until noodles are tender and cheese is melted. Let set for 5 minutes. Mix well again just before serving.

Each serving equals:

HE: 2 Protein • 2 Vegetable • 1 Bread •
5 Optional Calories

---

229 Calories • 5 gm Fat • 17 gm Protein •
29 gm Carbohydrate • 1,468 mg Sodium •
114 mg Calcium • 3 gm Fiber

DIABETIC: 2 Vegetable • 1½ Meat • 1½ Starch

Cabbage and Franks

This speedy skillet dish is the simplest kind of cooking I know—just pour in a few tasty ingredients, stir them together until they're "closelikethis," and let them simmer until their flavors are perfectly blended.   ☻   Serves 4 (1 cup)

> 8 ounces Healthy Choice 97% fat-free frankfurters, diced
> ½ cup chopped onion
> 3 cups shredded cabbage
> 1 (10¾-ounce) can Healthy Request Cream of Mushroom Soup
> 2 cups hot cooked noodles, rinsed and drained
> ⅛ teaspoon black pepper

In a large skillet sprayed with butter-flavored cooking spray, sauté frankfurters and onion for 5 minutes. Stir in cabbage. Continue cooking for 6 to 8 minutes or until cabbage is tender, stirring often. Add mushroom soup, noodles, and black pepper. Mix well to combine. Lower heat and simmer for 10 minutes, or until mixture is heated through, stirring occasionally.

HINTS: 1. 1¾ cups uncooked noodles usually cooks to about 2 cups.

2. Purchased coleslaw mix may be used in place of shredded cabbage.

Each serving equals:

HE: 1¾ Vegetable • 1⅓ Protein • 1 Bread •
½ Slider • 1 Optional Calorie

---

232 Calories • 4 gm Fat • 13 gm Protein •
36 gm Carbohydrate • 890 mg Sodium •
88 mg Calcium • 2 gm Fiber

DIABETIC: 2 Starch/Carbohydrate • 1 Vegetable •
1 Meat

Mediterranean Supper Skillet

I've heard that the nations who border the Mediterranean have low rates of heart disease, and I bet it's because their cuisine is more vegetable- than meat-based. This mouthwatering combo is a great summer supper solution, especially if you've got a garden full of ripe zucchini! ☻ Serves 4

2 cups chopped unpeeled zucchini
1 cup shredded carrots
½ cup chopped onion
2 (2.5-ounce) packages Carl Buddig 90% lean pastrami
1¾ cups (one 15-ounce can) Hunt's Chunky Tomato Sauce
½ cup (one 2.5-ounce jar) sliced mushrooms, drained
1 teaspoon Italian seasoning
1 teaspoon Sugar Twin or Sprinkle Sweet
¼ teaspoon black pepper
2 cups hot cooked noodles, rinsed and drained
¼ cup (¾ ounce) grated Kraft fat-free Parmesan cheese

In a large skillet sprayed with olive oil–flavored cooking spray, sauté zucchini, carrots, and onion for 5 minutes or until vegetables are just tender. Add pastrami, tomato sauce, mushrooms, Italian seasoning, Sugar Twin, and black pepper. Mix well to combine. Stir in noodles. Lower heat, cover, and simmer for 5 to 7 minutes, or until vegetables are tender, stirring occasionally. For each serving, place a full 1 cup of noodle mixture on a plate and sprinkle 1 tablespoon Parmesan cheese over top.

HINT: 1¾ cups uncooked noodles usually cooks to about 2 cups.

Each serving equals:

HE: 2 Vegetable • 1½ Protein • 1 Bread • 1 Optional Calorie

232 Calories • 4 gm Fat • 14 gm Protein • 35 gm Carbohydrate • 976 mg Sodium • 33 mg Calcium • 5 gm Fiber

DIABETIC: 3 Vegetable • 1½ Meat • 1 Starch

Pastrami Pizza Potatoes

Sometimes, when I'm not sure exactly what kind of dish I want to create, I just stir up a bunch of handy ingredients, bake them until they're done, and see what I get. This dish came about in part because I was looking for fun ways to use lean pastrami, I knew how much Cliff likes shredded potatoes, and I had just a little bit left of several different cheeses. Once you taste this luscious winner, you'll agree that my instincts led me in exactly the right direction!

● Serves 4

> 1¾ cups (one 15-ounce can) Hunt's Chunky Tomato Sauce
> 1½ teaspoons Italian seasoning
> 1 teaspoon Sugar Twin or Sprinkle Sweet
> ¼ cup (¾ ounce) grated Kraft fat-free Parmesan cheese
> ½ cup (one 2.5-ounce jar) sliced mushrooms, drained
> 1 (2.5-ounce) package Carl Buddig lean pastrami, shredded
> ⅓ cup (1½ ounces) shredded Kraft reduced-fat Cheddar cheese
> ⅓ cup (1½ ounces) shredded Kraft reduced-fat mozzarella cheese
> 3 cups (10 ounces) shredded loose packed frozen potatoes

Spray an 8-by-8-inch baking dish with olive oil–flavored cooking spray. In a large bowl, combine tomato sauce, Italian seasoning, Sugar Twin, and Parmesan cheese. Stir in mushrooms, pastrami, Cheddar cheese, and mozzarella cheese. Add potatoes. Mix well to combine. Spread mixture evenly into prepared baking dish. Cover and microwave on HIGH (100% power) for 15 minutes, turning after every 5 minutes. Let set for 2 to 3 minutes. Divide into 4 servings.

HINT: Mr. Dell's frozen shredded potatoes are a good choice for this recipe.

Each serving equals:

HE: 2 Vegetable • 1⅔ Protein • ¾ Bread • 1 Optional Calorie

194 Calories • 6 gm Fat • 13 gm Protein • 22 gm Carbohydrate • 1,241 mg Sodium • 173 mg Calcium • 4 gm Fiber

DIABETIC: 2 Vegetable • 2 Meat • 1 Starch

Making Healthy Exchanges Work for You

You're ready now to begin a wonderful journey to better health. In the preceding pages, you've discovered the remarkable variety of good food available to you when you begin eating the Healthy Exchanges way. You've stocked your pantry and learned many of my food preparation "secrets" that will point you on the way to delicious success.

But before I let you go, I'd like to share a few tips that I've learned while traveling toward healthier eating habits. It took me a long time to learn how to eat *smarter*. In fact, I'm still working on it. But I am getting better. For years, I could *inhale* a five-course meal in five minutes flat—and still make room for a second helping of dessert.

Now I follow certain signposts on the road that help me stay on the right path. I hope these ideas will help point you in the right direction as well.

1. **Eat slowly** so your brain has time to catch up with your tummy. Cut and chew each bite slowly. Try putting your fork down between bites. Stop eating as soon as you feel full. Crumple your napkin and throw it on top of your plate so you don't continue to eat when you are no longer hungry.

2. **Smaller plates** may help you feel more satisfied by your food portions *and* limit the amount you can put on the plate.

3. **Watch portion size.** If you are *truly* hungry, you can always add more food to your plate once you've finished your initial serving. But remember to count the additional food accordingly.

4. **Always eat at your dining-room or kitchen table.** You deserve better than nibbling from an open refrigerator or over the sink. Make an attractive place setting, even if you're eating alone. Feed your eyes as well as your stomach. By always eating at a table, you will become much more aware of your true food intake. For some reason, many of us conveniently "forget" the food we swallow while standing over the stove or munching in the car or on the run.

5. **Avoid doing anything else while you are eating.** If you read the paper or watch television while you eat, it's easy to consume too much food without realizing it, because you are concentrating on something else besides what you're eating. Then, when you look down at your plate and see that it's empty, you wonder where all the food went and why you still feel hungry.

Day by day, as you travel the path to good health, it will become easier to make the right choices, to eat smarter. But don't ever fool yourself into thinking that you'll be able to put your eating habits on cruise control and forget about them. Making a commitment to eat good healthy food and sticking to it takes some effort. But with all the good-tasting recipes in this Healthy Exchanges cookbook, just think how well you're going to eat— and enjoy it—from now on!

Healthy Lean Bon Appetit!

Recipe Index

I want to hear from you . . .

Besides my family, the love of my life is creating "common folk" healthy recipes and solving everyday cooking questions in *The Healthy Exchanges Way*. Everyone who uses my recipes is considered part of the Healthy Exchanges Family, so please write to me if you have any questions, comments, or suggestions. I will do my best to answer. With your support, I'll continue to stir up even more recipes and cooking tips for the Family in the years to come.

Write to: JoAnna M. Lund
c/o Healthy Exchanges, Inc.
P.O. Box 124
DeWitt, IA 52742

If you prefer, you can fax me at 1-319-659-2126 or contact me via e-mail by writing to HealthyJo@aol.com. (Or visit my Healthy Exchanges Internet web site at: http://www.healthyexchanges.com).

If you're ever in the DeWitt, Iowa, area, stop in and visit me at "The House That Recipes Built" and dine at **JO's Kitchen Cafe**, "Grandma's Comfort Food Made Healthy!"

JO's Kitchen™ Cafe
Grandma's Comfort Food Made Healthy!™
110 Industrial Street • DeWitt, Iowa 52742 • (319) 659-8234

Ever since I began stirring up Healthy Exchanges recipes, I wanted every dish to be rich in flavor and lively in taste. As part of my pursuit of satisfying eating and healthy living for a lifetime, I decided to create my own line of spices.

JO's Spices are salt-, sugar-, wheat-, and MSG-free, and you

can substitute them in any of the recipes calling for traditional spice mixes. If you're interested in hearing more about my special blends, please call Healthy Exchanges at 1-319-659-8234 for more information or to order. If you prefer, write to JO's Spices, c/o Healthy Exchanges, P.O. Box 124, DeWitt, IA 52742.

JO'S SPICES . . . A Healthy Way to Spice Up Your Life™

Now That You've Seen
Penny-Pinching Main Dishes,
Why Not Order
The Healthy Exchanges Food Newsletter?

If you enjoyed the recipes in this cookbook and would like to cook up even more of these "common folk" healthy dishes, you may want to subscribe to *The Healthy Exchanges Food Newsletter*.

This monthly 12-page newsletter contains 30-plus new recipes *every month* in such columns as:

- Reader Exchange
- Reader Requests
- Recipe Makeover
- Micro Corner
- Dinner for Two

- Crock Pot Luck
- Meatless Main Dishes
- Rise & Shine
- Our Small World

- Brown Bagging It
- Snack Attack
- Side Dishes
- Main Dishes
- Desserts

In addition to all the recipes, other regular features include:

- The Editor's Motivational Corner
- Dining Out Question & Answer
- Cooking Question & Answer
- New Product Alert
- Success Profiles of Winners in the Losing Game
- Exercise Advice from a Cardiac Rehab Specialist
- Nutrition Advice from a Registered Dietitian
- Positive Thought for the Month

Just as in this cookbook, all *Healthy Exchanges Food Newsletter* recipes are calculated in three distinct ways: 1) Weight Loss Choices, 2) Calories with Fat and Fiber Grams, and 3) Diabetic Exchanges.

The cost for a one-year (12-issue) subscription with a special Healthy Exchanges 3-ring binder to store the newsletters in is $28.50, or $22.50 without the binder. To order, simply complete the form and mail to us *or* call our toll-free number and pay with your VISA or MasterCard.

————— Yes, I want to subscribe to *The Healthy Exchanges Food Newsletter.* $28.50 Yearly Subscription Cost with Storage Binder $————

$22.50 Yearly Subscription Cost without Binder . . . . $————

————— Foreign orders please add $6.00 for money exchange and extra postage . . . . $————

————— I'm not sure, so please send me a sample copy at $2.50 . . . . $————

Please make check payable to HEALTHY EXCHANGES or pay by VISA/MasterCard

CARD NUMBER: _____   EXPIRATION DATE: _____

SIGNATURE: _____
         Signature required for all credit card orders.

Or Order Toll-Free, using your credit card, at 1-800-766-8961

NAME: _____

ADDRESS: _____

CITY: _____   STATE: _____ ZIP: _____

TELEPHONE:(___) _____

If additional orders for the newsletter are to be sent to an address other than the one listed above, please use a separate sheet and attach to this form.

MAIL TO: **HEALTHY EXCHANGES**
           P.O. BOX 124
           DeWitt, IA 52742-0124

           1-800-766-8961 for Customer Orders
           1-319-659-8234 for Customer Service

Thank you for your order, and for choosing to become a part of the Healthy Exchanges Family!